THE ROADMAP OF AL-MAHDI IN THE END TIMES

Decoding Prophecy, Systems, and the Restoration of Justice

SHAHJAHAN SIDDIQUI

First published 2026

Disclaimer: This book is grounded exclusively in authenticated Islamic sources — the Qur'an and the hadith tradition as classified by classical and contemporary hadith scholars. It does not claim to predict specific future events, identify living individuals with prophetic figures, or advocate for any political movement or group. All interpretations are analytical and scholarly in nature. Where scholarly disagreement exists, it is presented transparently. Weak (da'if) narrations, where referenced, are clearly labeled and are not used as primary evidence.

Book Name : The Roadmap of Al Mahdi In the End Times

ISBN Number : 978-93-5890-518-2

For every generation that held fast to what was real

when the world rewarded what was convenient.

For the seekers of truth who found the tradition —

and for those the tradition is still waiting to find.

PREFACE

The Need for a Saviour in an Age of Entropy

Something is wrong. Most people alive today feel it, even if they cannot name it precisely. Institutions that once commanded trust now produce cynicism. Information, available in quantities no previous generation could have imagined, has somehow made clarity harder to find. The richest civilisation in the history of the species cannot agree on what is true, what is just, or what a human life is for.

This is not a political observation. It is a civilisational one. And it is not new — though the particular shape it takes in the early twenty-first century is unprecedented in its speed, its scale, and the sheer complexity of the forces driving it. What is new is the depth of the disorientation: the sense, shared across ideological divides and cultural contexts, that the frameworks used to make sense of the world are not merely inadequate but are actively dissolving.

Philosophers call this a meaning crisis. Economists call it institutional failure. Political scientists call it democratic backsliding. Technologists call it information overload. Each label captures something real. None of them captures the whole picture. And none of them — this is the argument this book makes — possesses the integrative depth to explain why civilisations that reach extraordinary material peaks simultaneously lose the capacity to sustain justice, truth, or moral coherence.

The Islamic prophetic tradition does.

Not because it is the only tradition that addresses these questions — it is not. But because the eschatological framework transmitted by the Prophet Muhammad, peace be upon him, and preserved across fourteen centuries of rigorous scholarly tradition, describes the conditions of the present moment with a precision that no secular framework has approached. It names the collapse of authentic knowledge (rafa' al-'ilm). It describes the institutionalisation of betrayed trust (amanah). It identifies the specific quality of moral inversion — the period when the patient is called weak and the transgressor is called strong — as a terminal symptom of systemic failure. It maps, with the specificity of a diagnostician rather than the vagueness of a prophet, exactly what the world looks like when it has made what comes next inevitable.

This book is about what comes next.

More precisely, it is about the framework within which what comes next can be understood — not sensationally, not as a countdown clock to apocalypse, but analytically, as a coherent systemic sequence: the emergence of Al-Mahdi as the correction's initiating force; the appearance of the Dajjal as the deception system's maximum expression; the descent of Isa ibn Maryam as the final completion of truth over its counterfeit; and the subsequent events that close the testing environment of human history and prepare the world for its final accounting.

The book does not predict. It diagnoses. It does not speculate. It authenticates. It does not sensationalise. It analyses. Every narration cited as evidence is classified by the standards of classical hadith criticism — sahih, hasan, or da'if — and those classifications are transparent throughout. Where scholars have disagreed on matters of eschatological detail, that disagreement is presented honestly rather than papered over with false certainty.

What the book argues is this: that the End Times framework, read as a system rather than a story, possesses a diagnostic and prescriptive power that fourteen centuries of popular treatment and academic analysis have not fully realised. That the minor signs are not isolated prophecies but a connected map of civilisational degradation. That Al-Mahdi is not a political messiah but a systemic corrective. That the Dajjal is not merely a future individual but a present architecture. And that Isa ibn Maryam's return is not the beginning of something new but the completion of something that was always true.

This book was written for the scholar who feels the weight of a tradition that anticipated every crisis we now inhabit. For the parent who wonders what moral framework to hand to a child in a world where truth itself has become contested. For the seeker from any tradition — or no tradition — who has looked at the present moment and asked whether it has a structure, a meaning, and an end that makes sense of all its difficulty.

It does. That is what this book attempts to show.

Shahjahan Siddiqui

METHODOLOGY

The Algorithm of Verification

A Framework for Filtering Truth

A book about the End Times that does not begin with a rigorous account of how it handles its evidence is a book that has already failed its reader. The tradition of Islamic eschatology is, by any measure, one of the most extensively narrated and most extensively embellished bodies of religious knowledge in the world. Fourteen centuries of transmission, commentary, popular elaboration, political manipulation, and sincere but undisciplined piety have produced a corpus in which the rigorously authenticated and the freely fabricated sit side by side — often in the same lecture, the same booklet, and the same online video.

This book operates according to a two-part methodology that it applies consistently and transparently throughout.

Part One: Classical Hadith Criticism

The Islamic scholarly tradition developed, within the first two centuries of the hijri calendar, the most sophisticated pre-modern system for the verification of transmitted oral reports in human history. This system — the science of hadith — evaluates every narration across two dimensions: its chain of transmission (isnad) and the content of the report itself (matn).

The isnad evaluates the integrity, accuracy, and continuity of every transmitter in the chain from the Prophet, peace be upon him, to the collector who preserved it in writing. Transmitters are assessed for their moral character (adalah), their precision of memory (dabt), and the continuity of their contact with those from whom they transmitted. A chain with all transmitters meeting these criteria, without any break or weakness, produces a narration classified as Sahih — rigorously authenticated. A chain with minor weaknesses that do not fundamentally undermine reliability produces a narration classified as Hasan — well-attested. A chain with significant weaknesses produces a narration classified as Da'if — weak.

The matn analysis examines whether the content of a narration contradicts the Qur'an, contradicts more reliably authenticated narrations, or contains anachronistic elements inconsistent with the prophetic period.

This book applies these standards as follows: Sahih and Hasan narrations are cited as evidentiary proof. Da'if narrations, where they appear, are explicitly labeled as such and used only for contextual illustration — never as primary theological evidence. Fabricated narrations (mawdu') are not cited at all. The principal collections drawn upon are Sahih al-Bukhari, Sahih Muslim, Sunan Abu Dawood, Sunan al-Tirmidhi, Sunan Ibn Majah, and Musnad Ahmad, with grading attributed to established scholars including Ibn Hajar al-Asqalani, al-Nawawi, al-Albani, and Shu'ayb al-Arnaut where relevant.

The Qur'an and Hadith: Their Distinct Roles

The Qur'an and the authenticated hadith tradition function as complementary but categorically distinct sources in this book. The Qur'an is the primary, unmediated, textually preserved revelation — its authenticity is not subject to chain analysis in the way that hadith are, because its transmission is mutawatir (transmitted by so many people in every generation that fabrication is rationally excluded). Qur'anic verses are cited with surah name and ayah number throughout.

The hadith tradition provides the prophetic elaboration of Qur'anic principles and the specific narrations about eschatological figures and events that the Qur'an references but does not detail. Hadith are cited with collection, hadith number, and narrating companion where identifiable. Where a hadith's classification is disputed among scholars, both positions are presented.

Part Two: Systems Analysis

The second methodological pillar of this book is systems thinking — the application of frameworks from complex adaptive systems, feedback dynamics, and information theory to the understanding of how the conditions described in prophetic narrations interact, reinforce, and escalate.

This is not a foreign imposition on the Islamic tradition. The Qur'an itself repeatedly invites analytical reasoning: 'Do they not reflect?' (Surah Muhammad, 47:24). 'Will you not then use reason?' (Surah al-Baqarah, 2:44). The tradition of rational engagement with revelation — from al-Farabi and Ibn Rushd through al-Ghazali and Ibn Khaldun — has always recognised that divine guidance speaks to the same reality that rational analysis examines, and that the two are complementary rather than competing.

The specific systems concepts applied in this book include:

- **KEY SYSTEMS CONCEPTS APPLIED IN THIS BOOK**
- Entropy — The progressive degradation of order into disorder; in eschatological terms, the measurable moral and epistemic decline charted across the minor signs
- Feedback Loops — Self-reinforcing cycles in which one form of systemic failure amplifies another; identified in the mutual reinforcement of rafa' al-'ilm, amanah collapse, and moral inversion
- Bifurcation Points — Threshold moments at which a system under stress can no longer continue along its current trajectory; Al-Mahdi's bay'ah is the supreme historical bifurcation point
- Signal vs. Noise — The discipline of distinguishing genuine eschatological indicators (structural, global, irreversible) from pattern-matching errors driven by availability bias
- Information Entropy — The progressive loss of reliable, depth-carrying information within an epistemic system; the systems analogue to rafa' al-'ilm
- Attractor States — The organising principles around which a system reorganises after a bifurcation; adl (justice) as Al-Mahdi's attractor vs. zulm (oppression) as the Dajjal's

A note on what this methodology explicitly excludes: this book does not calculate dates, identify living individuals with prophetic figures, associate specific nations or governments with eschatological actors, or treat any contemporary political development as a definitive fulfilment of a specific sign. The tradition's deliberate silence on timing is respected as a mercy, not lamented as a gap. The value of the framework lies entirely in what it illuminates about conditions and orientation — not in what it predicts about calendar dates.

GLOSSARY

Understanding the Language of Fitan

The following terms appear throughout this book. Many are Arabic words that carry precise theological or technical meanings that no single English equivalent fully captures. They are defined here as they are used in this text.

Adl (عدل)

Justice in its most comprehensive sense — not merely legal equality but the placement of everything in its rightful position, given its due weight and station. The restoration of adl is the primary stated mission of Al-Mahdi in the authenticated narrations.

Amanah (أمانة)

Trust; the faithful discharge of responsibility. In Islamic ethical thought, amanah is the load-bearing infrastructure of social organisation — when it collapses, every other form of institutional failure follows. One of the most diagnostically significant minor signs is described as its systemic loss.

Ashraat al-Sa'ah (أشراط الساعة)

The signs of the Hour; the prophetic indicators that mark the approach of the Day of Judgement. Divided by classical scholars into minor signs (sughra) — gradual, cumulative, many already fulfilled — and major signs (kubra) — discrete, irreversible, and sequentially structured.

Bay'ah (بيعة)

The covenant of allegiance through which a community formally recognises the leadership of a ruler, pledging obedience in exchange for governance according to divine guidance and justice. Al-Mahdi's bay'ah — given to him between the Rukn and the Maqam in Makkah — is the eschatological bifurcation point at which the system's correction is formally initiated.

Dajjal (الدجال)

Literally: the deceiver, the impostor. Al-Masih al-Dajjal — the False Messiah — is the figure described across sahih hadith as the supreme human manifestation of organised deception, who will emerge with apparent supernatural powers and mislead the vast majority of people. In this book he is understood as both a specific future individual and a systemic force whose pre-terminal manifestations are already present in the world's information and social architecture.

Fitnah (فتنة)

Trial; strife; confusion; sedition. A multivalent term that encompasses personal moral testing, social conflict, epistemic confusion, and the organised disruption of just order. The End Times are described in many narrations as an era of multiplying and intensifying fitan — plural of fitnah.

Hasan (حسن)

A classification in hadith criticism denoting a narration whose chain of transmission has minor weaknesses that do not fundamentally undermine its reliability. Hasan narrations are accepted as valid evidence in Islamic jurisprudence and theology.

Isnad (إسناد)

The chain of transmission of a hadith narration — the list of transmitters through whom the report travelled from the Prophet, peace be upon him, to the collector. The evaluation of the isnad is the primary mechanism of hadith authentication.

Qist (قسط)

Equity; proportional fairness. Often paired with adl in prophetic descriptions of Al-Mahdi's mission: he will 'fill the earth with adl and qist after it has been filled with zulm and jawr.' Where adl describes justice as the correct placement of things, qist emphasises the proportional and equitable dimension of that placement.

Rafa' al-'Ilm (رفع العلم)

Literally: the withdrawal or lifting of knowledge. One of the most analytically significant minor signs — the progressive disappearance of genuine, depth-carrying scholarship through the death of scholars, replaced not by equivalent depth but by confident ignorance. The prophetic description of the mechanism (Sahih al-Bukhari, Hadith 100) maps with striking precision onto the contemporary epistemological condition.

Sahih (صحيح)

Rigorously authenticated. In hadith classification, a narration whose entire chain of transmission consists of transmitters meeting the criteria of moral integrity (adalah) and precision of memory (dabt), with full continuity in the chain and content free of contradiction with more reliable sources. Sahih narrations constitute the highest tier of hadith evidence.

Zulm (ظلم)

Oppression; injustice; wrong-placement. Etymologically, the placing of something in a position it does not rightfully occupy — the unworthy in authority, the false in the position of truth, the powerful where the righteous should stand. The entire catalogue of the minor signs is, in the framework of this book, a description of a civilisation practicing zulm at scale across every dimension of social life.

CONTENTS

Table of Contents

فَهَلْ يَنظُرُونَ إِلَّا السَّاعَةَ أَن تَأْتِيَهُم بَغْتَةً

فَقَدْ جَاءَ أَشْرَاطُهَا

Fa-hal yanthurūna illā al-sā'ata an ta'tiyahum baghtatan — faqad jā'a ashrāṭuhā

"Are they waiting for anything except that the Hour should come upon them suddenly? Its signs have already come."

— Qur'an — Surah Muhammad, 47:18

✦ ✦ ✦

CHAPTER ONE

The Architecture of the End: Why Prophecy Is a System, Not a Story

Imagine watching a master architect unroll a blueprint. At first glance, the lines seem overwhelming — a tangle of measurements, load-bearing walls, and structural dependencies. But the trained eye does not see chaos. It sees logic. Each element serves a purpose, each tension is calculated, and the entire edifice depends on specific sequences being followed in a specific order. Remove one load-bearing wall prematurely, and the structure collapses. Ignore the sequencing, and nothing stands.

This is the precise lens through which the figure of Al-Mahdi must be understood. He is not an isolated saviour descending from nowhere. He is the load-bearing wall in the divine architecture of the End Times — the systemic corrective that cannot appear before its structural preconditions are met. Islamic eschatology, read analytically, is not a dramatic screenplay of supernatural events. It is a blueprint: a connected system of forces, feedback loops, and irreversible thresholds, engineered to diagnose the terminal failure of civilizations that have abandoned justice, and to restore the equilibrium that falsehood perpetually disrupts.

Most popular treatments of End Times prophecy present Al-Mahdi, the Dajjal, and Isa ibn Maryam (Jesus, peace be upon him) as sequential characters in a divine thriller. This book takes a fundamentally different position: these are not characters. They are systemic forces — each representing a distinct phase in the collapse and recalibration of a civilization that has lost its moral and epistemic equilibrium.

> *For the believer, this is not an abstract framework. It is a mirror held up to their own moment in history — asking whether the conditions they are living through are the early tremors of a system approaching its breaking point.*

> *For a father raising children in a world where truth itself is unstable — where algorithms determine what is real and institutions have lost the authority to say otherwise — the prophetic framework is not theology. It is a survival map.*

I. What Prophecy Actually Is

There is a fundamental misreading that has plagued popular discourse on Islamic eschatology for generations: the confusion between prediction and diagnosis. A prediction is a forecast — it tells you what will happen. A diagnosis, by contrast, tells you what is already happening and what it will become if the underlying conditions remain unchanged. The Prophetic traditions (ahadith) concerning the End Times belong emphatically to the second category.

The Prophet Muhammad (peace be upon him) was not simply forecasting future events. He was describing the terminal symptoms of systemic failure — moral, spiritual, political, and epistemological — and the corrective mechanism that divine wisdom has ordained. This is why the signs of the Hour are not random curiosities. They are data points in a diagnostic framework.

> *The Hour will not be established until trust is lost, leadership is given to those unworthy of it, and killing becomes widespread.*

— Sahih al-Bukhari, Hadith 59

Each of these indicators — betrayal of trust (amanah), misallocation of authority, and normalization of violence — describes a civilization in entropy: a system that has exhausted its capacity for self-correction and is now accelerating toward collapse. The Quran frames this moral architecture with unambiguous clarity:

> إِنَّ اللَّهَ يَأْمُرُ بِالْعَدْلِ وَالْإِحْسَانِ وَإِيتَاءِ ذِي الْقُرْبَىٰ
> وَيَنْهَىٰ عَنِ الْفَحْشَاءِ وَالْمُنْكَرِ وَالْبَغْيِ

Inna Allaha ya'muru bil-'adli wal-ihsani wa-ita'i dhil-qurba...

> *"Indeed, Allah commands justice, good conduct, and giving to relatives, and forbids immorality, bad conduct, and oppression."*
>
> **Surah An-Nahl, 16:90**

This ayah is not merely a moral injunction. Read systemically, it defines the operating conditions of a healthy civilization: justice as structure, goodness as culture, and kinship-bonds as social fabric. Al-Mahdi's mission — as the prophetic narrations describe it — is the restoration of precisely these three conditions when their opposites have become dominant. The signs of the Hour are, in essence, the progressive dismantling of each element in this verse.

CONCEPT: Entropy in Social Systems

- Entropy = the gradual degradation of order into disorder
- In prophetic discourse: moral entropy precedes political collapse
- Sign accumulation = measurable degradation signals
- Al-Mahdi's emergence = reintroduction of corrective order (16:90 restored)

II. The Three-Phase System

Systems thinking teaches us that complex systems — whether biological, economic, or civilizational — do not simply break down. They move through recognizable phases: stability, stress, critical threshold, and either recalibration or terminal collapse. The End Times framework in Islamic eschatology maps with remarkable precision onto this model.

Phase One is the period of systemic stress and accumulation of the minor signs — the gradual erosion of values, the dilution of knowledge, the rise of deception as a social norm, and the fragmentation of communal bonds. This is not a dramatic rupture. It is a slow hemorrhage. It is the phase we currently inhabit, and its recognition demands neither panic nor passivity, but clear-eyed analysis.

Phase Two is the emergence of Al-Mahdi — the systemic corrective mechanism. His role is the reintroduction of justice (adl) as the organizing principle of governance and community. In systems language, he is the negative feedback loop that counters runaway deviation. He does not create a utopia ex nihilo; he restores the equilibrium that prior generations dismantled.

Phase Three is the peak of deception — the Dajjal — followed by the final correction through Isa ibn Maryam. The Dajjal represents not merely a singular figure, but a systemic force: the maximum amplification of deception, manipulation, and the inversion of truth. His elimination by Isa ibn Maryam is the final zeroing-out of the corrupted variable in the equation.

THE THREE-PHASE SYSTEM OF END TIMES

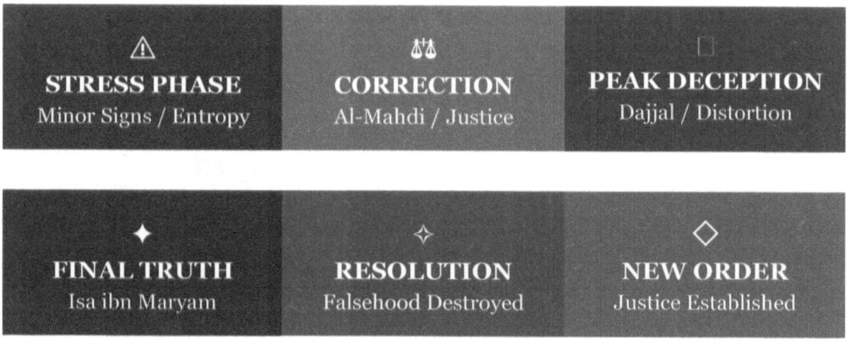

III. The Problem of Disconnected Narration

One of the most consequential scholarly failures in modern treatments of Islamic eschatology is the fragmentation of the prophetic narrative into isolated events. Al-Mahdi is discussed in one lecture. The Dajjal in another. Isa ibn Maryam in a third. The result is a collection of dramatic vignettes that generate emotional engagement but produce no analytical understanding.

This fragmentation mirrors the same epistemological crisis that plagues modern thought in general — the reduction of complex, interdependent phenomena into manageable but misleading units. In reality, the prophetic signs function as a single, integrated system. The behavior of one element influences the emergence of another.

The preconditions for Al-Mahdi's appearance are directly produced by the social and moral failures described in the minor signs.

> *There is no Mahdi except Isa ibn Maryam.*

— Ibn Majah, Sunan — Da'if narration (weak chain; cited for scholarly context only. Majority scholarly position, including Ibn Hajar al-Asqalani and Ibn Kathir, affirms Al-Mahdi as a distinct figure on the basis of sahih narrations)

The above narration is cited as an illustration of how isolated ahadith, stripped of chain analysis and systemic context, generate profound theological confusion. The narration is assessed as weak (da'if) by classical hadith critics. The majority scholarly consensus, based on mutawatir-level corroboration across the Sunan collections, affirms the Mahdi's distinct existence. Scholars differ on peripheral details — his precise lineage specification, the sequence of his emergence — but not on his fundamental role as affirmed across Sahih and Hasan narrations in Abu Dawood, Tirmidhi, and Musnad Ahmad.

> وَقُلْ جَاءَ الْحَقُّ وَزَهَقَ الْبَاطِلُ ۚ إِنَّ الْبَاطِلَ كَانَ زَهُوقًا
>
> *Wa qul jaa'a al-haqqu wa zahaqa al-batilu, inna al-batila kana zahuqa*
>
> *"And say: Truth has come, and falsehood has departed. Indeed, falsehood is ever bound to depart."*
>
> **Surah Al-Isra, 17:81**

This verse encodes the fundamental logic of the entire End Times system. Falsehood is not permanently viable — it carries within it the mechanism of its own dissolution. Al-Mahdi represents the human agency through which divine truth reclaims its structural dominance. The Dajjal is the final, maximum expression of zahuq al-batil — the convulsive last surge of falsehood before it collapses entirely under the weight of Isa ibn Maryam's return. The verse is not poetic reassurance. It is a systems law.

IV. The Secular Messiah: When Humanity Searches for Its Own Saviour

Here is a question secular modernity cannot answer honestly: if the concept of a divinely-sent restorer of justice is so primitive, so pre-rational, so irreconcilably mystical — then why does every civilization in every era produce an equivalent? Why does the 21st century, the most materially advanced in human history, not merely tolerate the idea of a coming saviour but actively manufacture new versions of it?

THE SECULAR MESSIAH

"Even in a world that rejects divine intervention, the search for a saviour persists — now redirected toward artificial intelligence, technological singularity, and utopian engineering."

The patterns are unmistakable:

AI as Omniscience: The belief that a sufficiently advanced AI will solve coordination failures, eliminate corruption, and optimize justice — replacing the need for moral leadership.

The Singularity as Resurrection: Ray Kurzweil and the transhumanist tradition promise a post-human threshold at which suffering, death, and inequality are algorithmically abolished.

The Tech Billionaire as Architect: Elon Musk, Sam Altman, and their peers are routinely cast — by themselves and their followers — as civilization-saviours operating outside the corrupt political system.

Effective Altruism as Prophethood: The EA movement explicitly frames its mission as calculating the optimal moral action to save the most future lives — a secular version of prophetic calculation.

The irony is precise and devastating. The same intellectual tradition that dismissed divine intervention as wishful thinking has rebuilt the entire architecture of messianism in secular materials. The names have changed. The emotional structure is identical: a broken world, a critical threshold approaching, and a singular force — technological, biological, or political — that will arrive and restore order.

The Islamic framework does not merely predict the arrival of Al-Mahdi. It predicts the failure of these secular substitutes and explains why they must fail. A system built on human ingenuity operating without divine justice as its axis cannot self-correct. The feedback loop is broken at the foundational level. Silicon cannot restore amanah. Algorithms cannot legislate taqwa. The Dajjal — the supreme deceiver — will in fact weaponize these very technologies, turning the tools of promised salvation into the instruments of mass manipulation.

> وَلَوْلَا دَفْعُ اللَّهِ النَّاسَ بَعْضَهُم بِبَعْضٍ لَّفَسَدَتِ الْأَرْضُ
>
> *Wa lawla dafu Allahi al-nasa ba'dahum biba'din lafasadati al-ard*
>
> *"And if it were not for Allah repelling some people by means of others, the earth would have been corrupted."*
>
> **Surah Al-Baqarah, 2:251**

This ayah articulates the divine mechanism of systemic correction with startling economy. Corruption, left unchecked, would consume the earth entirely. The correction is not inevitable through human ingenuity — it requires divinely-sanctioned agency. Al-Mahdi is precisely this: the human vessel of a correction that is systemic, ordained, and sequential. No secular equivalent — however sophisticated its engineering — operates within this framework. That is not a limitation of secular thought. It is, according to the prophetic tradition, precisely the vulnerability that the Dajjal will exploit.

> *For the young professional who has placed their faith in technology, in institutions, in the rational progress of civilization — this framework does not demand the abandonment of reason. It demands its completion.*
>
> *For the mother who watches her child absorb a thousand contradictory realities through a screen and wonders what anchors are left — the prophetic tradition offers not escapism, but orientation.*

V. Why This Framework Matters Now

The early 21st century presents a paradox that would have been unimaginable to previous generations: humanity has never been more connected, more literate, or more technologically capable — and simultaneously, institutional trust is collapsing globally, shared reality is fracturing, and the capacity for collective moral reasoning appears to be in acute decline.

Secular political philosophy responds with frameworks borrowed from economics, game theory, and behavioral psychology. Each offers partial insights but none possesses the integrative depth to explain why civilizations that reached extraordinary material peaks simultaneously lose the capacity to sustain justice, meaning, or social cohesion.

Al-Ghazali, writing in the eleventh century, understood that the crisis of his age was not primarily political or economic — it was epistemological. The confusion between knowledge and its counterfeit, between sincere scholarship and performative religiosity, was the root cause of civilizational vulnerability. The same diagnosis applies with striking precision to the present: artificial intelligence generates confident-sounding falsehoods, media ecosystems reward engagement over truth, and political movements exploit cognitive biases at industrial scale.

> وَأَشْرَقَتِ الْأَرْضُ بِنُورِ رَبِّهَا وَوُضِعَ الْكِتَابُ
>
> *Wa ashraqati al-ardu bi-nuri rabbiha wa wudi'a al-kitab*
>
> *"And the earth will shine with the light of its Lord, and the record of deeds will be placed."*
>
> **Surah Az-Zumar, 39:69**

This verse describes the ultimate resolution — the moment when divine light, not human engineering, reclaims the earth as its operating principle. The entire End Times system in prophetic narration moves toward this moment. Al-Mahdi's justice is its terrestrial prelude. Isa ibn Maryam's return is its celestial confirmation. The Dajjal's defeat is the removal of the final obstruction. Reading this verse after understanding the system does not feel like theology. It feels like watching a blueprint arrive at its final panel.

MODERN PARALLELS: Prophetic Diagnoses

- Rafa' al-'ilm (withdrawal of knowledge): Decline of deep

scholarship; viral misinformation replaces verified truth

- Al-hawa (desire-led reasoning): Algorithmic confirmation bias; post-truth political discourse
- Kathrat al-harj (proliferation of killing): State and non-state violence normalization globally
- Taqarub al-zaman (time compression): Acceleration culture; attention collapse; 24-hour news cycle
- Istifadat al-mal (wealth amid injustice): Record inequality alongside record GDP — precisely 16:90 inverted

---

VI. Method: How This Book Reads the Evidence

This book applies a disciplined dual methodology. The first is classical hadith criticism — the science of evaluating prophetic narrations through the integrity of their chains (isnad) and the coherence of their content (matn). Only sahih and hasan narrations will be presented as evidentiary proof. Where da'if narrations appear, they will be explicitly labeled and used only for contextual illustration.

The second methodology is systems analysis — drawing on complex adaptive systems, feedback dynamics, and emergence to understand how the conditions described in prophetic narrations interact, reinforce, and escalate. This is not an imposition of alien intellectual categories onto Islamic theology. The Quran itself repeatedly invites analytical reasoning: 'Do they not reflect?' (Surah Muhammad, 47:24); 'Will you not then use reason?' (Surah Al-Baqarah, 2:44).

Where scholars have differed on matters of eschatological detail — and differences exist on questions ranging from the sequence of the major signs to the precise geography of events — this book will present the scholarly debate transparently, without manufacturing false certainty. The goal is not another sensationalist roadmap to the apocalypse. It is the kind of structured, evidence-based understanding that transforms passive observers into people capable of moral clarity in confusing times.

> *Whoever among you sees an evil, let him change it with his hand; if he cannot, then with his tongue; if he cannot, then with his heart — and that is the weakest of faith.*
>
> — **Sahih Muslim, Hadith 49**

This hadith encodes a principle of systemic intervention: injustice operates at multiple levels simultaneously — institutional, discursive, and attitudinal — and meaningful response requires calibrated engagement at each level. Al-Mahdi's mission, as examined in subsequent chapters, operates at all three levels simultaneously. That is precisely what makes his role, in the prophetic framework, structurally irreplaceable.

> *For the scholar who has spent years in the texts and feels the weight of a tradition that anticipated every crisis we now inhabit — this book is not a summary. It is an invitation to see the architecture you already know in its full, connected depth.*

The Question This Book Asks

The central question animating this work is deceptively simple: If the prophetic tradition provides a comprehensive framework for understanding civilizational collapse and restoration, why does most engagement with it produce either passive fatalism or fringe sensationalism — and almost never the kind of grounded, actionable wisdom it was clearly designed to produce?

The answer lies in the failure to read prophecy as a system. Once that shift is made — once the reader stops asking 'when will this happen?' and starts asking 'what conditions produce these outcomes, and what does their presence or absence tell us?' — the entire tradition opens up with an analytical power that rivals any secular framework for understanding historical change.

Al-Mahdi is not simply coming. He is, in the prophetic architecture, the point at which a civilization that has generated sufficient justice-seeking critical mass finally produces the figure capable of translating that potential into structural reality. Understanding what produces that critical mass, what destroys it, and what the forces arrayed against it actually look like — that is the work of this book.

> *For those who still believe that justice is possible in this world — not as an ideal, but as a lived, structural reality — the prophetic tradition does not offer comfort. It offers something far more demanding: a map.*

The question is no longer whether the system will collapse —

but whether we will recognize the signs before the correction arrives.

✦ ✦ ✦

Chapter Two: The Science of Signs — Reading the Minor Portents as a System

continues on the following page...

CHAPTER TWO
The Science of Signs:
Reading the Minor Portents as a System

A seismologist does not wait for the earthquake to study the earth. Long before the ground ruptures, she reads the tremors — the micro-fractures accumulating beneath the surface, the pressure differentials building in fault lines no eye can see. The earthquake, when it arrives, surprises no one who was paying attention. It surprises only those who mistook the absence of visible collapse for the presence of structural health.

The minor signs of the Hour function with precisely this logic. They are not curiosities scattered through prophetic narration as dramatic decoration. They are the seismic record of a civilization fracturing at its moral and epistemic foundations — pressure readings accumulating across decades and centuries, each one measurable, each one pointing toward the same irreversible threshold. The question the Prophet Muhammad (peace be upon him) was answering, through these signs, was not: 'What will the apocalypse look like?' It was: 'What does a world that has made the apocalypse inevitable look like — and how will you know when you are living in it?'

> *For anyone paying attention to the world in the early 21st century — the institutional collapses, the epistemic chaos, the exhaustion of meaning — this chapter is not prophecy.*

> *It is a diagnosis of the present moment, written fourteen centuries ago.*

I. Two Categories, One System

Classical Islamic scholarship has consistently divided the signs of the Hour into two categories: the minor signs (ashraat al-sa'ah al-sughra) and the major signs (ashraat al-sa'ah al-kubra). This division is not merely organizational. It encodes a critical systemic distinction: the minor signs are the causal inputs, while the major signs are the systemic outputs. One category produces the conditions; the other emerges from them.

The major signs — the emergence of Al-Mahdi, the appearance of the Dajjal, the descent of Isa ibn Maryam, the rising of the sun from the West, Gog and Magog, and others — do not arrive randomly. They arrive when the minor signs have collectively pushed the system past a critical threshold of moral and social entropy. This is why studying the minor signs in isolation, as if each were a separate prophecy to be checked off a list, fundamentally misses the point. Their significance is cumulative and systemic.

> فَهَلْ يَنظُرُونَ إِلَّا السَّاعَةَ أَن تَأْتِيَهُم بَغْتَةً ۖ فَقَدْ جَاءَ
> أَشْرَاطُهَا

Fa-hal yanthuruna illa al-sa'ata an ta'tiyahum baghtatan, faqad ja'a ashratuha

"Are they waiting for anything except the Hour to come upon them suddenly? Its signs have already come."

Surah Muhammad, 47:18

The Quran's use of the word ashraat — signs, forerunners — is deeply precise. It does not say 'its sign' (singular) but 'its signs' (plural), indicating that the Hour is preceded by a constellation of indicators, not a single dramatic herald. The prophetic elaboration of these signs is therefore not supplementary to the Quranic framework — it is its systematic unpacking.

SYSTEM DISTINCTION: Minor vs Major Signs

- Minor Signs = Causal inputs → Gradual, accumulating, many already fulfilled
- Major Signs = System outputs → Irreversible, sequential, each triggers the next
- Relationship: Minor signs create conditions; major signs emerge from them
- Error to avoid: Reading major signs without understanding their minor sign preconditions
- Al-Mahdi's emergence = First major sign; requires full accumulation of minor-sign entropy

II. The Architecture of the Minor Signs

The Prophet Muhammad (peace be upon him) described dozens of minor signs across authenticated narrations. Scholars including Ibn Kathir in Al-Nihayah, al-Suyuti in Al-Jami' al-Saghir, and Ibn Hajar al-Asqalani in Fath al-Bari have catalogued, analyzed, and classified these narrations with meticulous care. What emerges from a systemic reading of this scholarly tradition is not a random list, but a coherent degradation map — a progression through five distinct categories of systemic failure.

These five categories do not operate in strict sequence. They operate as simultaneous, mutually reinforcing feedback loops — each category of failure accelerating the deterioration of the others. This is the hallmark of complex systems in collapse: no single cause, but a web of causes each amplifying the rest.

THE FIVE CATEGORIES OF SYSTEMIC MINOR SIGNS

1 — EPISTEMOLOGICAL COLLAPSE
Withdrawal of knowledge (rafa' al-'ilm) · Rise of ignorance · Proliferation of false scholars

⚖ **2 — INSTITUTIONAL CORRUPTION**
Authority given to the unworthy · Trust (amanah) abandoned · Leaders who do not lead

💬 **3 — SOCIAL FRAGMENTATION**
Severing of kinship ties · Normalization of betrayal · Neighborhood blindness

□ **4 — MATERIAL DISTORTION**
Abundance of wealth alongside injustice · Architectural extravagance · Competition in worldly display

⚡ **5 — MORAL INVERSION**
The patient is called weak · The transgressor is called strong · Good is called evil and evil good

---

III. Rafa' al-'Ilm — The Withdrawal of Knowledge

Of all the minor signs, the withdrawal of authentic knowledge is perhaps the most analytically significant — because it is the root cause from which the other four categories of failure grow. A civilization that loses its capacity for truthful, rigorous scholarship loses its immune system. Every subsequent pathology becomes, in its absence, inevitable.

> *Allah does not take away knowledge by snatching it from the people's hearts, but He takes it away by the death of the scholars, until no scholar remains. Then people will take ignorant persons as their leaders; they will be asked questions and will give religious verdicts without knowledge, going astray and leading others astray.*

— **Sahih al-Bukhari, Hadith 100; Sahih Muslim, Hadith 2673**

The mechanism described in this hadith is critical and frequently misread. The knowledge is not taken suddenly. It is not erased from books or forbidden by decree. It dies gradually, through the death of scholars who carry it in their hearts — scholars whose passing is not replaced by equivalent depth, only by equivalent confidence. The successors know the vocabulary of knowledge without its substance. They can speak its language fluently and lead others astray with complete sincerity.

This is the epistemological crisis the modern world has industrialized. The internet did not create the problem of false authority — it scaled it. A person with three million followers and a confident delivery now functions, for their audience, as a scholar, a scientist, a theologian, or a philosopher — regardless of whether they have invested the intellectual labor that any of those titles requires. The hadith describes this not as a technological accident but as a systemic inevitability when genuine depth is no longer cultivated.

> *For the student who spent years studying, only to find their carefully researched positions drowned out by viral half-truths — this hadith is not just consolation. It is confirmation that the erosion they are witnessing has a name, a mechanism, and a trajectory already mapped.*

IV. The Trust Collapse — Amanah as Social Infrastructure

The concept of amanah — trust, reliability, the faithful discharge of one's responsibilities — functions in Islamic ethical thought as the load-bearing infrastructure of social organization. When amanah is intact, institutions function, agreements hold, and the gap between public role and private reality is narrow. When amanah collapses, the opposite of each becomes true: institutions hollow out while maintaining their exterior forms, agreements become strategic performances, and public authority is exercised in service of private interest.

> *When amanah is lost, then wait for the Hour. It was asked: How will it be lost, O Messenger of Allah? He said: When authority is given to those who do not deserve it.*

— Sahih al-Bukhari, Hadith 59

The diagnostic precision of this hadith is extraordinary. It does not say authority will be seized by force — though it sometimes is. It says it will be given — entrusted — to those unworthy of it. This describes a process of institutional decay far more insidious than simple corruption: a civilization that has lost the capacity to distinguish competence from performance, genuine moral authority from its mimicry. The selection mechanisms themselves have been corrupted.

In systems terms, this represents the failure of the feedback loop that normally corrects misallocation of authority. Healthy systems have mechanisms — cultural, institutional, electoral, scholarly — that identify and remove incompetent or corrupt leadership. When those mechanisms degrade, the system loses its self-correcting capacity. Bad decisions accumulate rather than being reversed. Institutions that should serve the public begin serving themselves. The exterior form of authority persists while its substance evaporates.

> إِنَّ اللَّهَ يَأْمُرُكُمْ أَن تُؤَدُّوا الْأَمَانَاتِ إِلَىٰ أَهْلِهَا وَإِذَا
> حَكَمْتُم بَيْنَ النَّاسِ أَن تَحْكُمُوا بِالْعَدْلِ
>
> *Inna Allaha ya'murukum an tu'addu al-amanati ila ahliha wa idha hakamtum bayna al-nasi an tahkumu bil-'adl*
>
> *"Indeed, Allah commands you to render trusts to whom they are due, and when you judge between people, to judge with justice."* **Surah An-Nisa, 4:58**

This verse encodes the twin pillars of social health: amanah (trusts rendered to their rightful owners) and adl (justice in judgment). Al-Mahdi's prophesied mission is the simultaneous restoration of both — a recalibration of the system back to this Quranic baseline after generations of progressive deviation. The minor signs are the map of that deviation. Al-Mahdi is its correction.

V. Signal vs. Noise — The Modern Reading Problem

One of the most significant analytical challenges in engaging with the minor signs is the problem of false identification: the tendency to see every contemporary crisis as a prophetic fulfillment, and every historical upheaval as the definitive threshold. This has produced, across Muslim intellectual history, a recurring pattern of premature eschatological certainty — each generation convinced that their specific moment of crisis is the final moment.

This pattern is not random. It reflects a deep human cognitive bias: the availability heuristic, which causes us to weight recent, vivid, emotionally salient events as more significant than the base rate of history warrants. Every generation has experienced institutional corruption, moral decline, and social fragmentation. Every generation has had legitimate reasons to identify their era as the one described in prophetic narration. The fact that most were wrong does not mean the signs are not real — it means the reading methodology requires more discipline.

SIGNAL vs. NOISE: A DISCIPLINED READING FRAMEWORK

✓ SIGNAL (Genuine Fulfillment)	✕ NOISE (False Identification)
Qualitative AND quantitative shift — not just 'some increase' but structural transformation	Every war is 'kathrat al-harj' · Every leader is 'unworthy' · Every decline is 'rafa al-ilm'
Globally widespread, not locally observed — the sign describes civilizational, not regional, collapse	Local crises projected onto global prophetic templates without scale analysis
Cross-referencing multiple signs accumulating simultaneously as a cluster	Single-sign identification without systemic pattern confirmation
Aligned with scholarly analysis across multiple madhhabs and traditions	Driven by emotional salience or political convenience of the identification
Irreversible quality — the condition, once established, does not self-correct	Cyclical phenomenon mistaken for terminal condition

The disciplined approach is to look not for isolated matches but for cluster patterns — multiple categories of systemic failure manifesting simultaneously, globally, and with an irreversible character. This is what distinguishes legitimate eschatological analysis from what Ibn Khaldun would have recognized as the perennial human tendency to inflate the significance of one's own moment.

> *For the reader scanning this list and mentally checking boxes — 'yes, yes, this is happening, this too' — the discipline required is not to suppress that recognition but to subject it to rigorous analysis rather than emotional confirmation. The prophetic tradition demands both the recognition and the rigor.*

VI. The Compression Signs — Time, Distance, and Acceleration

Among the most analytically striking minor signs are those that describe a subjective or structural transformation in the experience of time and distance. The Prophet Muhammad (peace be upon him) described a period when time would feel compressed — when a year would pass like a month, a month like a week, a week like a day. For centuries, this narration was read as purely subjective or spiritual in character. The 21st century has given it a more literal resonance.

> *The Hour will not be established until time becomes short, a year passes like a month, a month like a week, a week like a day, a day like an hour, and an hour like the burning of a palm-leaf.*
>
> **— Musnad Ahmad, Hadith 10560 — Hasan**

The cognitive psychology literature has a name for this phenomenon: time acceleration, or time famine — the subjective sense that time is moving faster than one can manage, driven by information density, decision overload, and the fragmentation of attention. What previous generations experienced as a stable, spacious temporal reality has, in the era of smartphones, 24-hour news cycles, and always-on communication, transformed into exactly the compressed, breathless quality the hadith describes.

This is not to claim that technological time compression is what the hadith refers to — scholars differ, and the ultimate referent may be eschatological in a way that transcends sociological explanation. But the resonance is worth analytical attention. A civilization in which attention spans collapse, in which the depth required for genuine knowledge becomes structurally harder to cultivate, is a civilization in which both amanah and 'ilm erode by default — without any active malice required. The system degrades itself.

> وَمَا يُدْرِيكَ لَعَلَّ السَّاعَةَ تَكُونُ قَرِيبًا
>
> *Wa ma yudrīka la'alla al-sa'ata takoonu qarīban*
>
> *"And what will make you perceive? Perhaps the Hour is near."* **Surah Al-Ahzab, 33:63**

VII. The Moral Inversion — When Good Is Called Evil

The most sophisticated category of minor signs — and the most analytically challenging — is what might be termed the moral inversion cluster: narrations describing a period when the prevailing social consensus systematically misidentifies virtue as weakness and transgression as strength. This is not simply a period of moral decline. It is a period of moral disorientation — when the metrics themselves are corrupted.

> *There will come a time when the one who holds fast to his religion will be like one holding a burning coal.*
>
> **— Sunan al-Tirmidhi, Hadith 2260 — Sahih**

The diagnostic weight of this hadith is not in its description of physical suffering but in what produces that suffering: a social environment in which religious integrity has become socially costly — where fidelity to moral truth requires not intellectual effort but social courage, because the social penalty for holding fast is real. This is a precise description of a civilization in which moral inversion is not merely present but institutionalized — embedded in the social reward and punishment structures that shape behavior.

Modern behavioral science has a framework for this: preference falsification, developed by economist Timur Kuran. In environments where the social cost of expressing a genuine moral preference is high, individuals publicly perform the preferred social position while privately maintaining different convictions. Over time, this produces a civilization of systematic moral inauthenticity — where what is publicly affirmed bears decreasing relationship to what is privately believed, and where the social consensus is therefore not a measure of genuine conviction but of coordinated performance.

The connection to the minor signs is direct and measurable. When moral authenticity carries social cost, scholarship becomes performative, leadership becomes theatrical, and the institutions designed to transmit truth begin transmitting what is socially rewarded instead. This is how epistemological collapse, institutional corruption, and moral inversion form a single, mutually reinforcing feedback loop — the three most diagnostically significant clusters of minor signs all operating as one system.

> *For the person who feels the weight of holding a position they know to be true in a room where everyone performs the opposite — this hadith is not a spiritual abstraction. It is a recognition: you are not confused. The environment is inverted. The burning coal is real.*

VIII. The Aggregation Threshold — Are We There?

This is the question most readers arrive at by this point, and intellectual honesty requires engaging it directly rather than deflecting into methodological caution. The answer, based on a rigorous systems-based reading of authenticated narrations and contemporary conditions, is: the minor signs are not merely being fulfilled in isolated instances. Multiple categories are fulfilling simultaneously, globally, and with an irreversible structural character.

The withdrawal of authentic knowledge is not a regional complaint — it is a global epistemological crisis, driven by the collapse of institutional authority, the democratization of confident-sounding misinformation, and the replacement of depth with reach as the primary credential. The trust collapse is not a cultural peculiarity — it is measured across every major institutional category in every Pew Research, Edelman Trust Barometer, and global governance survey of the past three decades. The moral inversion is not a polemical observation — it is the measurable, documented outcome of preference falsification operating at scale across social, political, and educational systems.

What remains uncertain — and scholars across the tradition have been appropriately cautious here — is the precise timing and triggering sequence. The accumulation of minor signs creates the systemic pressure. The emergence of Al-Mahdi is the systemic response to that pressure reaching a critical threshold. At what exact point that threshold is crossed, no human analysis can determine with certainty. What can be determined is the direction of travel, the rate of acceleration, and the structural conditions that the prophetic tradition identifies as the necessary preconditions.

> *Signs will follow one another like the beads of a rosary when the string breaks.*
>
> **— Musnad Ahmad — narration classified Hasan by contemporary hadith scholars including al-Arnaut**

The image is precise and systemic: not a steady stream, not a sudden flood, but an accelerating cascade — each sign releasing the next, the intervals shortening, the cumulative weight growing until the string breaks and what was sequential becomes simultaneous. This is the threshold model of systemic collapse: gradual accumulation followed by rapid, non-linear acceleration. The world does not drift to its eschatological threshold slowly and evenly. It accelerates.

AGGREGATION ANALYSIS: Current Sign Clusters

- Epistemological (Rafa' al-'ilm): Globally active — institutional knowledge authority in structural decline
- Trust/Amanah: Globally active — documented across every institutional category since the 1970s
- Social fragmentation: Globally active — loneliness epidemic, kinship dissolution, community atomization
- Material distortion: Globally active — record wealth concentration alongside record human displacement
- Moral inversion: Contextually active — varies by social environment; institutionally accelerating in many societies
- Compression signs: Cognitively active — attention collapse, time famine, information overload documented globally

---

The Preconditions Are the Point

A common misreading of the minor signs treats them as obstacles to overcome — things to wait out before the 'real' eschatological drama begins with the major signs. This inverts the actual logic. The minor signs are the point. They are the civilization's self-diagnosis, made available in advance for those with the analytical tools to read it accurately. Their accumulation is not incidental to Al-Mahdi's emergence — it is its cause.

Al-Mahdi does not arrive to rescue a world that does not know it is broken. He arrives when the fractures have become undeniable, when the systemic failures have produced sufficient suffering and disillusionment that the restoration of justice becomes, for the first time in generations, genuinely desired rather than merely invoked rhetorically. The minor signs, in this reading, are not a countdown clock. They are the story of how humanity loses and then recovers its capacity to want what is right.

> وَنُرِيدُ أَن نَّمُنَّ عَلَى الَّذِينَ اسْتُضْعِفُوا فِي الْأَرْضِ
> وَنَجْعَلَهُمْ أَئِمَّةً
>
> *Wa nuridu an namunna 'ala alladhina istud'ifu fi al-ardi wa naj'alahum a'immatan*
>
> *"And We desired to confer favor upon those who were oppressed in the land and make them leaders."*
>
> **Surah Al-Qasas, 28:5**

This verse — revealed in the context of the oppression of Banu Israel and the emergence of Musa (Moses, peace be upon him) — is cited by scholars including Ibn Kathir and al-Qurtubi as a universal principle of divine correction: that periods of systemic oppression and moral collapse are precisely the preconditions from which the divinely-ordained correction emerges. The minor signs describe the oppression. Al-Mahdi's emergence enacts the principle of this verse. The connection is structural, not merely metaphorical.

> *For the believer living through the weight of these accumulating signs — feeling simultaneously that history is accelerating beyond comprehension and that the frameworks for understanding it are dissolving — this verse is not comfort. It is orientation. Oppression of this scale is not the absence of divine attention. It is its prelude.*

The minor signs are not the story of what is ending.

They are the story of what must break before justice can be rebuilt.

✦ ✦ ✦

Chapter Three: The Man and the Mission — Who Is Al-Mahdi?

continues on the following page...

CHAPTER THREE

The Man and the Mission:

Who Is Al-Mahdi?

History records a recurring figure — not supernatural, not infallible, but appearing at precisely the moment when a collapsing civilization produces, from within its own suffering, the leader capable of absorbing its weight and redirecting its momentum. Umar ibn al-Khattab did not emerge from comfort. Salahuddin al-Ayyubi did not appear during stability. The figure the historical record consistently confirms is forged in the conditions that make their mission necessary — and arrives, not ahead of those conditions, but because of them.

Al-Mahdi is this logic taken to its ultimate expression. He is not a supernatural interruption of history. He is history's deepest corrective impulse made incarnate — a man, born into the world's entropy, who carries within him the capacity to restore what centuries of systemic failure have dismantled. Understanding him begins not with his miraculous attributes, but with his authenticated identity: who the prophetic tradition actually describes, with what textual precision, on the authority of which scholars, and with what degree of analytical certainty.

This chapter does what too few treatments of Al-Mahdi attempt: it separates the rigorously authenticated from the embellished, the scholarly consensus from the peripheral disputes, and the prophetic portrait from the political projections that have, across fourteen centuries, been layered over it by those who found it convenient to claim — or to manufacture — a Mahdi.

> *For the sincere Muslim who has heard Al-Mahdi's name invoked to justify movements, leaders, and revolutions that later proved to be fraudulent or catastrophic — this chapter is a recalibration. The authentic portrait is more grounded, more human, and ultimately more powerful than any of its counterfeits.*

I. The Hadith Evidence — What Is Actually Authentic

The first and most critical task is establishing what the authenticated prophetic narrations actually say about Al-Mahdi — and distinguishing that firmly from the accretions, fabrications, and misattributions that have accumulated in popular discourse. The hadith sciences offer a precise methodology for this, and the classical scholars have applied it with admirable rigor.

The core narrations regarding Al-Mahdi are distributed across the major hadith collections. The most authoritative cluster includes narrations in Sunan Abu Dawood, Sunan al-Tirmidhi, Sunan Ibn Majah, and Musnad Ahmad. It is a point of frequent confusion that the two most widely known collections — Sahih al-Bukhari and Sahih Muslim — do not contain explicit narrations naming Al-Mahdi by that title. This has led some scholars to question the authenticity of the concept entirely. The response of the hadith sciences is instructive.

> *Al-Mahdi is from my progeny, from the children of Fatimah.*

— Sunan Abu Dawood, Hadith 4284 — Sahih according to al-Albani and al-Arnaut

> *The world will not pass away until a man from my family, whose name will be the same as mine, rules over the Arabs.*

— Sunan al-Tirmidhi, Hadith 2230 — Hasan Sahih according to al-Tirmidhi

> *Al-Mahdi will emerge at the end of my Ummah. Allah will send rain for him, the earth will bring forth its vegetation, wealth will be distributed equitably, livestock will increase, and the Ummah will be great. He will live for seven or eight years.*

— Mustadrak al-Hakim, Hadith 8578 — Sahih according to al-Hakim; al-Dhahabi concurred

The cumulative weight of these narrations — assessed across chains of transmission by scholars including al-Suyuti, Ibn Kathir, Ibn Hajar al-Asqalani, and in the modern era by al-Albani and Shu'ayb al-Arnaut — reaches the level of mutawatir bil-ma'na: transmitted by so many independent chains, with such consistency of core meaning, that collective fabrication is rationally excluded. The concept of Al-Mahdi as a coming restorer from the Prophet's family is among the most robustly authenticated elements of Islamic eschatological belief.

HADITH AUTHENTICATION SUMMARY

- Sunan Abu Dawood 4284: Sahih — narrated by Umm Salamah (RA), authenticated by al-Albani
- Sunan Tirmidhi 2230: Hasan Sahih — narrated by Ibn Masood (RA), confirmed by al-Tirmidhi
- Mustadrak al-Hakim 8578: Sahih — narrated by Abu Sa'id al-Khudri (RA)
- Musnad Ahmad 1:376: Multiple chains — collectively elevate narrations to Hasan li-ghayrihi
- Scholarly verdict: Al-Mahdi's existence = confirmed by scholarly ijma' (consensus) based on mutawatir chains
- NOT in Bukhari/Muslim by name — but absence ≠ rejection; both contain related narrations on justice restoration

II. The Authenticated Portrait — What the Narrations Describe

Once the authentic narrations are assembled and cross-referenced, a coherent portrait emerges. It is not a portrait of a superhuman figure. It is the portrait of a specific human being, carrying specific inherited qualities, emerging under specific historical conditions, and executing a specific mission — with divine facilitation, not divine replacement of human agency.

AL-MAHDI: AUTHENTICATED PROFILE

Name Muhammad ibn Abdullah — same first and paternal name as the Prophet (pbuh)	**Lineage** Descendant of the Prophet (pbuh) through Fatimah al-Zahra, from the Hasani or Husayni line (scholars differ on which branch; both are narrated)
Physical Description Broad forehead, prominent (aquiline) nose — described in Abu Dawood and Tirmidhi narrations	**Character at Emergence** Does not seek leadership; reluctant to accept the role; confirmed by popular acclaim, not self-proclamation
Location of Emergence Makkah al-Mukarramah — between the Rukn and Maqam, at the time of his pledging of allegiance (bay'ah)	**Duration of Leadership** Seven, eight, or nine years — narrations vary; scholars note this may refer to different phases of his mission
Mission Fill the earth with justice and equity (qist wa adl) after it had been filled with oppression and tyranny (zulm wa jawr)	**Relationship to Isa (pbuh)** Prays behind Isa ibn Maryam when Isa descends — Al-Mahdi leads the Muslims; Isa follows his lead in prayer

Several elements of this portrait deserve analytical attention. First: the reluctance. Every authenticated narration that addresses Al-Mahdi's emergence describes a man who does not seek the role. The bay'ah — the pledge of allegiance that formally establishes his leadership — is given to him by others, in Makkah, under circumstances described in the narrations as involving a period of social chaos and competing claimants. This reluctance is not incidental to his character. It is, in the prophetic framework, a defining qualification. A Mahdi who seeks the title has, by that seeking, disqualified himself.

Second: the specificity of the mission. The narrations do not describe Al-Mahdi as establishing a caliphate in the administrative sense, building an empire, or restoring a particular political structure. They describe him as filling the earth with adl and qist — justice and equity — after it had been filled with their opposites. This is a systemic description, not a political one. The emphasis is on the quality of the social order he produces, not the institutional form through which he produces it.

> وَعَدَ اللَّهُ الَّذِينَ آمَنُوا مِنكُمْ وَعَمِلُوا الصَّالِحَاتِ
> لَيَسْتَخْلِفَنَّهُمْ فِي الْأَرْضِ
>
> *Wa'ada Allahu alladhina amanu minkum wa 'amilu al-salihati layastakhlifannahum fi al-ard*
>
> *"Allah has promised those who have believed among you and done righteous deeds that He will surely grant them succession upon the earth."*
>
> **Surah An-Nur, 24:55**

Classical mufassirun — including Ibn Kathir, al-Tabari, and al-Qurtubi — identify this verse as containing within it the principle that finds its ultimate eschatological expression in Al-Mahdi's emergence. The promise of succession (istikhlaf) to those who believe and act righteously is not a historical observation about early Muslim governance alone. It is a divine law: that justice-seeking communities, when they reach sufficient moral coherence, become the vehicle through which Allah restores equitable order to the earth. Al-Mahdi is the named, specific instantiation of this divine law at the end of the systemic cycle.

III. The Scholarly Disputes — Where Differences Exist

Intellectual honesty demands that the genuine scholarly disputes around Al-Mahdi's identity and emergence be presented clearly. These disputes do not undermine the authenticated core — they clarify its boundaries. Understanding where scholars agree and where they differ is itself a form of analytical rigor that popular treatments consistently fail to provide.

DISPUTED ELEMENT	POSITIONS HELD	SCHOLARLY WEIGHT
Hasani or Husayni lineage	Some narrations specify the Hasani branch; others point to Husayni. Both chains exist.	Majority lean Hasani based on Abu Dawood's narration chain; Ibn Kathir acknowledges both
Duration of his rule	Seven years (Tirmidhi), eight years (Muslim — related narration), nine years (Abu Dawood variant)	Al-Nawawi suggested the variation reflects different phases; not a contradiction
Geographic location of emergence	Consensus: Makkah. Some narrations suggest he comes from Madinah or Khurasan (East).	Emergence is in Makkah; his origin may be elsewhere — not contradictory readings
Whether the Mahdi is Isa himself	Ibn Majah narration (da'if): 'No Mahdi except Isa.' Weak chain; rejected by majority.	Classified da'if by Ibn Hajar; majority scholarly consensus affirms a distinct Mahdi figure
Is belief in Al-Mahdi obligatory?	Scholars of Ahl al-Sunnah: Affirming Al-Mahdi is wajib based on mutawatir narrations.	Ibn Khaldun's skepticism is a minority position; countered comprehensively by al-Suyuti

Ibn Khaldun's famous skepticism toward the Mahdi narrations in his Muqaddimah deserves particular attention, as it is frequently cited by modernist Muslim thinkers as a license to dismiss the concept entirely. Ibn Khaldun's critique was methodological — he found the individual chains weak. Al-Suyuti's comprehensive response in Al-'Urf al-Wardi fi Akhbar al-Mahdi demonstrated that Ibn Khaldun had examined chains individually rather than cumulatively. When the narrations are assessed collectively — as mutawatir bil-ma'na — the picture changes entirely. The scholarly community, from Ibn Hajar to contemporary hadith scholars including Shu'ayb al-Arnaut, has consistently upheld the cumulative authenticity.

> *For the intellectually honest reader troubled by the variation in narrations — this variation is not a weakness of the tradition. It is the tradition working as designed: preserving multiple chains, allowing scholarly cross-referencing, and resisting the flattening of nuance into false certainty. The disputes are features of a living intellectual tradition, not cracks in its foundation.*

IV. The False Mahdis — A History of Counterfeits

Perhaps no aspect of the Al-Mahdi tradition has caused greater historical damage than the phenomenon of false Mahdis — individuals who claimed, or were attributed, the title of Al-Mahdi for political, revolutionary, or messianic purposes. Analyzing these cases is not merely historical curiosity. It is an essential component of understanding the authentic portrait, because each false Mahdi fails in precisely the ways that the authenticated portrait predicts he would.

HISTORICAL FALSE MAHDIS — SYSTEMIC ANALYSIS

Muhammad Ahmad al-Sudani (d. 1885) — Declared himself Al-Mahdi in Sudan. Led a successful military revolution, established a state, died of typhus 6 months after his greatest victory. Sought the title actively; self-proclaimed.

Muhammad ibn Tumart (d. 1130) — Founder of the Almohad movement; his followers attributed Al-Mahdi status to him. Scholarly credentials were genuine; the political attribution was not. His successors produced a dynasty, not justice.

Juhayman al-Utaybi (1979) — Seized the Grand Mosque in Makkah, proclaiming his brother-in-law as Al-Mahdi. Ended in catastrophic military confrontation; the claimed Mahdi was killed in the siege. Active self-seeking of role; violent emergence — opposite of the authentic portrait.

Mirza Ghulam Ahmad (d. 1908) — Claimed multiple messianic titles including Mahdi. Founded the Ahmadiyya movement. Claimed prophethood after Muhammadhood; rejected by unanimous scholarly consensus as heretical.

COMMON FAILURE PATTERN: Every false Mahdi shares one or more of three characteristics the authentic narrations explicitly exclude: self-proclamation, political seeking of the role, or violent seizure of authority.

The pattern of false Mahdis illuminates the authentic portrait with negative precision. Each claimant fails where the authentic narrations are most specific: Al-Mahdi does not seek the role — the false Mahdis invariably do. Al-Mahdi is acclaimed by others in Makkah — the false Mahdis declare themselves, or are declared, in contexts of political convenience. Al-Mahdi's mission produces justice and equity as measurable social outcomes — the false Mahdis produced, at best, temporary political order and, at worst, sectarian catastrophe.

The analytical lesson is not cynicism about the concept. It is precision about the criteria. The false Mahdi phenomenon actually strengthens the case for the authentic portrait's coherence: the tradition is specific enough to generate falsifiable predictions, and every historical claimant has been falsifiable against them.

> بَلْ نَقْذِفُ بِالْحَقِّ عَلَى الْبَاطِلِ فَيَدْمَغُهُ فَإِذَا هُوَ زَاهِقٌ
>
> *Bal naqdhifu bil-haqqi 'ala al-batili fa-yadmaghuhu fa-idha huwa zahiq*
>
> *"Rather, We hurl truth against falsehood, and it destroys it, and thereupon it departs."*
>
> **Surah Al-Anbiya, 21:18**

The Quran's description of truth's relationship to falsehood — not gentle displacement but decisive demolition — applies to the counterfeit Mahdi phenomenon with particular force. Each false Mahdi, however compelling their initial momentum, is eventually 'zahiq' — utterly departed. The authentic Al-Mahdi, by contrast, is not merely prophesied to appear. He is prophesied to be succeeded by Isa ibn Maryam himself — the ultimate validation that no counterfeit can approximate.

V. Al-Mahdi as Systemic Corrective — Not Political Messiah

The most consequential reframing this book argues for is the shift from understanding Al-Mahdi as a political messiah — a sovereign who establishes an Islamic state — to understanding him as a systemic corrective: a human mechanism through which divine justice recalibrates a civilization that has been systematically driven away from its moral axis.

This distinction has profound implications. The political messiah model generates a set of expectations: military victory, territorial expansion, the establishment of specific institutional forms, the resolution of geopolitical conflicts. These expectations, when imported into the reading of prophetic narrations, produce a distorted portrait — one that emphasizes the dramatic and spectacular at the expense of the substantive and systemic.

The systemic corrective model generates a different set of expectations — ones that map far more precisely onto the authenticated narrations. Al-Mahdi's primary achievement, as described consistently across the sahih and hasan hadith, is not territorial: it is distributive. Wealth is shared equitably. Rain comes. The earth produces. Livestock multiply. These are descriptions of a restored ecological and economic equilibrium — a society that has recovered its capacity to organize itself around sufficiency and justice rather than accumulation and exploitation.

> *He will distribute wealth without counting it. A man will come to him and say: Give me, give me. He will give him all that he can carry in his garment.*

— Sahih Muslim, Hadith 2913 — narrated in the context of the righteous leader before the end; classical scholars including al-Nawawi connect this to the Mahdi tradition

This hadith is analytically striking. The description of wealth distribution 'without counting' does not describe a political program.

It describes the restoration of a moral posture toward material resources — a civilization that has recovered from hoarding, accumulation, and the institutionalized anxiety of scarcity into one operating from genuine abundance of spirit as much as material. This is a systemic outcome, not a policy achievement. It requires a transformation of the social organism, not merely its political structures.

> *For the economist or policy analyst reading this — the description of equitable distribution, agricultural abundance, and livestock increase is not fairy tale. It is the description of a civilization that has solved the coordination problem that every just society has always faced: aligning individual incentive with collective welfare. The prophetic tradition says this problem is solved, once, at the end — and describes its resolution not as a technocratic achievement but as a moral one.*

AL-MAHDI'S MISSION: SYSTEMIC vs. POLITICAL

- Political model (incorrect): Military conqueror, state-builder, geopolitical actor
- Systemic model (authenticated): Moral recalibrator, justice restorer, equilibrium-reinstaller
- Primary narrated achievement: Wealth distributed equitably — structural transformation, not policy
- Secondary achievements: Agricultural abundance, livestock increase — ecological restoration
- Duration: 7-9 years — sufficient for systemic correction, not empire-building
- Succession: Prays behind Isa ibn Maryam — his mission prepares conditions for the final correction

---

VI. The Emergence Conditions — What Produces Al-Mahdi

One of the most analytically rich aspects of the Al-Mahdi narrations is what they reveal about the conditions of his emergence.

These conditions are not merely dramatic backdrop. They are the causal inputs in the system — the specific configuration of social reality that the prophetic tradition identifies as both necessitating and enabling Al-Mahdi's appearance.

> *There will be a caliph in the last period of my Ummah who will freely give handfuls of wealth to the people without counting it. And before him will be great turmoil.*
>
> **— Sahih Muslim, Hadith 2914**

The phrase 'great turmoil' before Al-Mahdi is not vague dramatic seasoning. The Arabic harj wa marj — used across narrations — describes a specific quality of social chaos: the breakdown of stable authority, the collapse of the social contract, competing claims to leadership, and the exhaustion of populations who can no longer identify a trustworthy institutional anchor. It is the description of a civilization that has consumed its social capital and arrived at the point of maximum institutional bankruptcy.

This is the precise systemic condition from which Al-Mahdi emerges — not as its cause, but as its response. The population, exhausted by counterfeit leadership and institutional betrayal, is for the first time genuinely ready to receive authentic justice rather than merely invoke it rhetorically. Al-Mahdi does not impose justice on a resistant population. He offers it to a population that, having lived through its absence long enough, has developed the moral coherence to recognize and sustain it.

> *People will come from the East carrying black banners. They will ask for good things but will not be given them. They will fight and will be victorious... When you see them, give them your allegiance, even if you have to crawl over ice.*
>
> **— Sunan Ibn Majah, Hadith 4084 — Da'if according to al-Albani; cited for context only, not as proof**

The above narration is flagged explicitly as da'if and is included only to illustrate the category of emergence-condition narrations that populate popular eschatological discourse. Its weakness does not reflect on the authenticated narrations — it illustrates the importance of hadith criticism. The emergence conditions that are authentically narrated are sufficient for the analytical picture:

systemic chaos, exhaustion of false authority, and the emergence of a figure unwilling to seek but impossible to refuse.

> وَلَقَدْ كَتَبْنَا فِي الزَّبُورِ مِن بَعْدِ الذِّكْرِ أَنَّ الْأَرْضَ
> يَرِثُهَا عِبَادِيَ الصَّالِحُونَ
>
> *Wa laqad katabna fi al-Zaburi min ba'di al-dhikri anna al-arda yarithuha 'ibadiya al-salihun*
>
> *"And We have already written in the Psalms, after the mention of the Torah, that the earth is inherited by My righteous servants."*
>
> **Surah Al-Anbiya, 21:105**

Al-Qurtubi, in his tafsir of this verse, identifies it as one of the Quranic anchors for the eschatological restoration of just governance — a divine inscription, present across revelatory traditions, that the righteous will ultimately inherit the earth's governance. Al-Mahdi's emergence is, in this reading, not an Islamic sectarian claim but the fulfillment of a cross-traditional divine promise — one that the Quran explicitly locates also in the Zabur (Psalms). This comparative dimension has significant implications for how the tradition speaks across religious boundaries, and will be explored further in subsequent chapters.

VII. The Human Dimension — A Man Who Did Not Choose This

There is a quality in the authenticated portrait of Al-Mahdi that is rarely dwelt upon but is perhaps the most humanly significant: he does not want it. The narrations are consistent and specific about this. He is a man living his life when circumstances converge around him. The bay'ah is given — pressed upon him — between the Rukn and the Maqam in Makkah. He accepts because he cannot not accept. The weight of the world's need, and the divine appointment that channels it, does not ask his preference.

This is not a detail of dramatic flavor. It is a theologically and psychologically precise portrait of how genuine leadership — the kind that actually produces justice rather than merely performing it — is structured. The man who desperately wants to lead is optimizing for the experience of leadership. The man who accepts reluctantly, because the need is real and he is the one who can serve it, is optimizing for the mission. These are not the same person, and they do not produce the same outcomes.

> *For anyone who has ever been asked to carry a weight they did not choose — a responsibility they did not seek but could not refuse because the need was real and they were the one present — the portrait of Al-Mahdi is not distant theology. It is a recognition of the deepest structure of genuine service.*

The prophetic tradition consistently honors this quality. The Prophet Muhammad (peace be upon him) himself, in multiple sahih narrations, expressed his preference for a simple life over the burden of prophethood — while accepting it completely because the mission demanded acceptance. Umar ibn al-Khattab wept when given the caliphate, understanding its weight. The pattern is not coincidental. The tradition is encoding a principle: the capacity to bear the mission without being seduced by its power is itself a qualification for the mission.

> *Al-Mahdi is from us, Ahl al-Bayt. Allah will reform him in a single night.*

— **Sunan Ibn Majah, Hadith 4085 — Hasan according to al-Busiri; authenticated by al-Albani**

The phrase 'Allah will reform him in a single night' has generated significant scholarly discussion. The majority reading, following Ibn Kathir and al-Suyuti, is that this refers to a divine preparation or ripening — a moment of spiritual and psychological clarity in which the man becomes fully ready for the mission. It is not a description of a supernatural personality transplant. It is the description of a threshold moment in which human readiness and divine facilitation converge. Every great mission in prophetic history has had such a moment: the cave of Hira, the night of Isra wal-Mi'raj, the moment Musa stood before the burning bush. The night of Al-Mahdi's preparation is in this tradition.

The Portrait and Its Power

What emerges from a rigorous, authenticated, analytically disciplined study of the Al-Mahdi narrations is a portrait significantly more powerful than the popular mythology surrounding the figure — precisely because it is more human, more specific, and more structurally coherent.

He is a man, not a myth. He carries a specific name, a specific lineage, a specific physical description, and a specific character disposition — reluctance being the most diagnostic. He emerges under specific conditions: the exhaustion of false authority, the collapse of institutional trust, the desperate readiness of a population for genuine justice. He executes a specific mission: the restoration of adl and qist as the operational principles of social organization. And he operates within a specific systemic context: as the first major corrective in a three-phase sequence that culminates in the descent of Isa ibn Maryam and the final defeat of the Dajjal.

The false Mahdis have always tried to replicate the dramatic exterior of this portrait while lacking its interior qualities. They have sought what he will not seek. They have proclaimed what he will not proclaim. They have built what he will not build — empires, movements, dynasties — when his mission, authenticated and specific, is something far more difficult and far more enduring: the restoration of justice as a lived, structural reality in a world that has forgotten what it feels like.

> *For the generation living through the accumulation of minor signs described in the previous chapter — watching institutions hollow out, truth fragment, and justice become a rhetorical device rather than an operational principle — the portrait of Al-Mahdi is not an escape into prophecy. It is a reminder that the system has a correction built into it. And that the correction will be human, reluctant, specific, and real.*

Al-Mahdi does not arrive to give the world what it wants.

He arrives to give it what, after everything, it finally deserves.

✦ ✦ ✦

Chapter Four: The Bay'ah — The Moment the System Shifts

continues on the following page...

CHAPTER FOUR
The Bay'ah —
The Moment the System Shifts

There is a category of historical moments that systems theorists call bifurcation points — instants at which a system under accumulated stress reaches the threshold where it can no longer continue along its current trajectory and must either collapse entirely or reorganize at a higher level of complexity and coherence. These moments are rarely visible as they happen. They are recognized, almost always, only in retrospect — as the hinge on which everything turned.

The bay'ah of Al-Mahdi is, in the prophetic architecture of the End Times, the supreme bifurcation point in human civilizational history. It is the moment at which the accumulated entropy of the minor signs — centuries of institutional decay, epistemic collapse, trust betrayal, and moral inversion — reaches the threshold from which spontaneous self-correction becomes impossible, and a divinely-facilitated, humanly-executed correction becomes not merely necessary but inevitable. Everything before the bay'ah is the system breaking. Everything after it is the system being rebuilt.

This chapter examines what the authenticated prophetic narrations actually describe about the bay'ah — its setting, its circumstances, its immediate context of chaos, and its world-historical meaning. It then situates that description within the broader systemic framework this book has been building: understanding the bay'ah not as a dramatic scene in an eschatological screenplay, but as the precise structural mechanism through which a civilization's self-correcting capacity is restored after total failure.

> *For anyone who has lived through the moment when a dysfunctional institution — a company, a family, a community — finally breaks past the point of patching and requires a complete reset: you already understand the emotional logic of the bay'ah. The question is whether the reset produces something better, or merely different chaos. The prophetic tradition answers that question with extraordinary specificity.*

I. What Is Bay'ah — The Covenant as System Mechanism

The Arabic word bay'ah derives from the root ba-ya-'a — to sell, to exchange, to seal a transaction. In Islamic political theology, the bay'ah is the formal covenant of allegiance between a leader and the community they serve: the community offers its obedience and support; the leader accepts the responsibility of governance in accordance with justice and divine guidance. It is simultaneously a contractual, spiritual, and political act — encoding the mutual obligation that lies at the heart of legitimate Islamic governance.

The Quran addresses the bay'ah directly in the context of the early Muslim community's pledge to the Prophet Muhammad (peace be upon him):

> إِنَّ الَّذِينَ يُبَايِعُونَكَ إِنَّمَا يُبَايِعُونَ اللَّهَ يَدُ اللَّهِ فَوْقَ
> أَيْدِيهِمْ

Inna alladhina yubayo'unaka innama yubayo'una Allaha, yadu Allahi fawqa aydihim

"Indeed, those who pledge allegiance to you — they are actually pledging allegiance to Allah. The hand of Allah is over their hands."

Surah Al-Fath, 48:10

This verse establishes a theological principle that extends directly to the bay'ah of Al-Mahdi: the covenant of legitimate leadership is not merely a political agreement between human parties. It is a transaction in which divine sanction is the ultimate guarantor. The hand of Allah over the hands of those pledging — yad Allah fawqa aydihim — encodes the reality that a genuine bay'ah carries a weight that no political calculation can simulate and no counterfeit Mahdi can replicate. This is why the false Mahdis analyzed in Chapter Three all failed at this precise point: their bay'ahs were transactions between political actors, not covenants sealed under divine sanction.

In systems terms, the bay'ah functions as the moment of phase transition: the point at which the system formally reorganizes under new operating principles. Before the bay'ah, the old system — however degraded — is the operative reality. After the bay'ah, a new attractor state begins to exert its pull on the system's trajectory. The transition is not instantaneous in its effects, but it is instantaneous in its structural significance. The bifurcation point has been crossed.

BAY'AH AS SYSTEMIC MECHANISM

- Pre-Bay'ah state: Maximum entropy — competing false authorities, institutional bankruptcy, population exhaustion
- Bay'ah moment: Phase transition — divine sanction meets human covenant; new attractor state established
- Post-Bay'ah trajectory: System begins reorganizing around justice (adl) as primary operating principle
- Key distinction: Legitimate bay'ah = divinely sanctioned, community-initiated, reluctantly accepted
- Counterfeit bay'ah = politically engineered, self-sought, enthusiastically accepted — opposite signature
- Quranic anchor: Surah Al-Fath 48:10 — the hand of Allah seals the covenant

II. The Setting — Makkah at the Breaking Point

The authenticated narrations are remarkably specific about the setting of Al-Mahdi's bay'ah. It occurs in Makkah al-Mukarramah — the most sacred geography in Islamic tradition — at a moment of acute social and political crisis. The specificity is not incidental. Makkah is the center of the world's spiritual gravitational field in Islamic cosmology. That the system's correction is anchored there encodes a profound theological statement: the restoration of justice begins at the point where the human relationship with the divine is most concentrated.

> *A man will come to Makkah. The people of Makkah will bring him out of his home even though he is unwilling. They will give him the bay'ah between the Rukn and the Maqam.*

— Sunan Abu Dawood, Hadith 4286 — Sahih according to al-Albani

Three elements of this narration deserve careful analytical attention. First: the phrase 'brought out from his home' — he is not presenting himself publicly, not campaigning, not building a movement. He is in his home when the events come to him. This is the definitive marker of authenticity that distinguishes Al-Mahdi from every historical pretender: the role finds him, not the reverse.

Second: 'even though he is unwilling' — the Arabic kariha, meaning aversion or reluctance, is unambiguous. This is not performative humility — the kind that says 'I don't want this' while clearly pursuing it. The narrations describe genuine reluctance, requiring the community to insist and Al-Mahdi to ultimately yield not to ambition but to obligation.

Third: the precise location — between the Rukn (the Black Stone corner of the Ka'bah) and the Maqam Ibrahim. This is not a general description of Makkah. It is a specific sacred geography, whose significance in Islamic spiritual tradition is profound. The bay'ah occurs at the most sanctified spot within the most sanctified place on earth. Its legitimacy is anchored in the earth's own holiness.

> *For the Muslim who makes Tawaf and stands between the Rukn and the Maqam in their own worship — the knowledge that this precise location will one day witness the covenant that restores justice to the world transforms a personal devotional act into a participation in something whose scope extends beyond any individual life. The geography of worship becomes the geography of history's turning point.*

III. The Chaos Before the Covenant — Harj wa Marj

The prophetic narrations do not describe Al-Mahdi's bay'ah as emerging from a calm, deliberate process of community discernment. They describe it emerging from a period of acute, cascading social and political crisis — what the Arabic tradition calls harj wa marj: the convergence of killing, confusion, and the collapse of legitimate authority across multiple competing claimants.

> *There will be turmoil (fitna) in which people will be like riding animals — whoever they encounter, they trample. The Syrian follows his Syrian leader; the Iraqi follows his Iraqi leader. At that, a man from Quraysh whose maternal uncles are from Kalb will appear... then Al-Mahdi will emerge.*

— Sunan Abu Dawood, Hadith 4285 — Hasan according to al-Albani

The imagery in this hadith — people like riding animals, trampling whoever they encounter — is a description of social atomization at its most extreme: a state in which the shared frameworks that make coordinated, civilized existence possible have dissolved, leaving only the logic of power, faction, and survival. What the hadith describes is not merely political conflict. It is the complete breakdown of the social contract.

The competing regional leaderships — Syrian, Iraqi — represent the fragmentation of authority into mutually hostile, geographically bounded power centers, each claiming legitimacy without the capacity to produce it. This pattern — competing claims, regional fragmentation, populations forced to choose sides in conflicts that serve none of them — is precisely the systemic condition that the minor signs described in Chapter Two predict as the terminal stage of institutional decay.

THE CONVERGENCE SEQUENCE — FROM CHAOS TO BAY'AH

① **MAXIMUM HARJ WA MARJ**

Competing false authorities — regional fragmentation — social contract dissolved

Abu Dawood 4285 — Hasan

② **ARMY FROM THE EAST (KHURASAN)**

An army advances carrying banners — interpreted by scholars as a precursor signal to Al-Mahdi's emergence

Various narrations — scholarly disagreement on precise identity; treated as contextual

③ **AL-MAHDI IN SECLUSION IN MAKKAH**

He is in his home, not seeking, not campaigning — the role has not yet found him publicly

Abu Dawood 4286 — Sahih

④ **COMMUNITY BRINGS HIM OUT**

The people of Makkah — or a group of the believers — compel him to accept; he resists

Abu Dawood 4286 — Sahih

⑤ **BAY'AH — BETWEEN RUKN AND MAQAM**

The covenant of allegiance is sealed at the most sacred geography on earth; the phase transition occurs

Abu Dawood 4286 — Sahih; Tirmidhi 2230 — Hasan Sahih

⑥ **SUFYANI ARMY SENT TO OPPOSE HIM**

An opposing army advances toward Makkah — is swallowed by the earth at al-Bayda' — a major sign

Sahih Muslim 2882 — the sinking of the army

IV. The Army That Sinks — The First Divine Confirmation

Among the narrations surrounding Al-Mahdi's bay'ah, one of the most analytically significant — and most rigorously authenticated — is the account of the army sent to suppress him that is swallowed by the earth in the desert. This event, described in Sahih Muslim, functions within the systemic framework as the first decisive divine confirmation of the bay'ah's legitimacy: the moment at which the universe itself registers that the bifurcation point has been crossed and the old order's attempt to restore itself will not succeed.

> *An army will advance against the Ka'bah and when it reaches al-Bayda' — a place between Makkah and Madinah — the earth will swallow them from the first to the last.*
>
> **— Sahih Muslim, Hadith 2882 — narrated by Aisha (RA)**

The authenticity of this narration is beyond scholarly dispute — it resides in Sahih Muslim, the second most authoritative hadith collection in Sunni Islam. What requires analytical attention is its systemic significance. The army advancing against the Ka'bah represents the last organized attempt of the collapsing old order to suppress the correction that the bay'ah has set in motion. That it is swallowed by the earth — rather than defeated militarily — encodes a precise theological statement: this correction is not a political revolution that can be countered by a superior army. It is a divinely-guaranteed systemic reorganization that no human force can reverse once the bay'ah threshold has been crossed.

Scholars have debated whether this army is specifically the Sufyani's forces, a general Roman or tyrannical force, or another entity. Ibn Kathir, al-Nawawi, and al-Suyuti discuss the narration's context extensively in their respective works on the End Times. The scholarly differences concern the identity of the army, not the authenticity or meaning of the event itself. What is unanimous is the event's significance as the first major miraculous confirmation of Al-Mahdi's legitimacy following the bay'ah.

> وَإِذَا أَرَدْنَا أَن نُّهْلِكَ قَرْيَةً أَمَرْنَا مُتْرَفِيهَا فَفَسَقُوا فِيهَا
> فَحَقَّ عَلَيْهَا الْقَوْلُ فَدَمَّرْنَاهَا تَدْمِيرًا

Wa idha aradna an nuhlik qaryatan amarna mutrafiyaha fafasaqu fiha fahaqqa 'alayha al-qawlu fad ammarnaaha tadmira

"And when We intend to destroy a city, We command its affluent ones and they defiantly disobey therein; so the word of punishment is justified against it, and We destroy it with total destruction."

Surah Al-Isra, 17:16

This verse articulates the divine law of civilizational destruction: the command comes to the affluent and powerful — those with the greatest capacity to maintain justice — and their transgression justifies the verdict. The army advancing against Al-Mahdi represents precisely this dynamic: power that had the capacity to support justice choosing instead to suppress it. The earth's swallowing of that army is the execution of the divine verdict. In this reading, the miraculous event is not an interruption of the natural order but its ultimate expression.

V. The Sufyani — The Counter-System

No analysis of the bay'ah and its immediate context is complete without engaging the figure of the Sufyani — one of the most consistently narrated yet analytically complex elements of the pre-Mahdi period. The Sufyani represents, within the systemic framework of this book, the counter-corrective: a force that rises in the same period of systemic chaos as Al-Mahdi, but whose purpose is the perpetuation of tyranny rather than its removal.

> *The Sufyani will emerge from the depth of Damascus. Most of his followers will be from the tribe of Kalb. He will kill until he rips open the wombs of women and kills children. Then Qays will gather against him and he will kill them until not one rider survives. A man from my family will emerge in the Haram...*

— Sunan Abu Dawood, Hadith 4287 — Da'if according to al-Albani; cited for contextual framework only

The above narration is flagged as da'if and included solely for contextual illustration of the Sufyani framework. The concept of the Sufyani as an opponent of Al-Mahdi is supported across multiple narration chains, including stronger narrations in other collections, and scholars of hadith including Ibn Kathir and al-Suyuti have written extensively on the cumulative evidence. The individual chain above is weak, but the concept is supported by the broader hadith corpus.

What makes the Sufyani analytically significant is not his biographical details but his structural role. In a period of maximum systemic chaos, two competing forces emerge simultaneously: one oriented toward the restoration of justice (Al-Mahdi), one oriented toward the consolidation of tyranny (the Sufyani). This is precisely the dynamic that systems theory predicts at bifurcation points: competing attractors vying to capture the reorganizing system. The outcome is determined not by the balance of military power alone but by which force carries the greater structural integrity — which, in the prophetic framework, is determined by divine sanction.

AL-MAHDI	THE SUFYANI
Emerges reluctantly — brought out by the community	Emerges actively — rises through military aggression
From the Prophet's family — Ahl al-Bayt lineage	Descendant of Abu Sufyan — historical opposition lineage
Bay'ah in Makkah — most sacred geography	Emerges from Damascus — center of political-military power
Mission: Fill earth with justice (adl wa qist)	Mission: Consolidate power through terror and killing
Divine confirmation: Army sent against him is swallowed	Divine verdict: His army is destroyed; he is eventually killed
Systemic role: Corrective attractor — reorganizes system upward	Systemic role: Entropic attractor — attempts to perpetuate collapse

VI. Al-Mahdi's Leadership — Justice as Operating System

Once the bay'ah is sealed and the immediate counter-forces are neutralized — the Sufyani's army swallowed, the chaos of competing claims resolved — the narrations shift from the drama of emergence to the substance of Al-Mahdi's mission. What does his governance actually look like? What does the restoration of justice mean in operational terms? The authenticated hadith describe not a political manifesto but a social ecosystem — a lived reality of material abundance, equitable distribution, and restored natural harmony.

> *My Ummah will be blessed during the time of Al-Mahdi with a blessing the like of which they have never experienced before. The sky will rain abundantly upon them, the earth will not withhold any of its vegetation, and wealth will be in piles. A man will stand up and say: O Mahdi, give me! He will say: Take.*

— Mustadrak al-Hakim, Hadith 8578 — Sahih according to al-Hakim; concurred by al-Dhahabi

The description here is not primarily economic. It is ecological and moral simultaneously. 'The sky will rain abundantly' and 'the earth will not withhold its vegetation' are not merely meteorological observations. In the Quranic framework, environmental abundance and human moral order are directly linked — rain and vegetation are among the blessings that flow from a community living in alignment with divine principles, and their withdrawal is among the signs of collective moral failure.

> وَلَوْ أَنَّ أَهْلَ الْقُرَىٰ آمَنُوا وَاتَّقَوْا لَفَتَحْنَا عَلَيْهِم بَرَكَاتٍ مِّنَ السَّمَاءِ وَالْأَرْضِ

Wa law anna ahla al-qura amanu wa-ittaqu lafatahna 'alayhim barakatin mina al-sama'i wa al-ard

"And if only the people of the cities had believed and feared Allah, We would have opened upon them blessings from the heaven and the earth."

Surah Al-A'raf, 7:96

This verse makes the causal relationship explicit: collective iman and taqwa produce material blessings from heaven and earth. Al-Mahdi's era is not described as a supernatural intervention that produces abundance despite human moral failure. It is the natural outpouring of abundance that occurs when a civilization has, through Al-Mahdi's corrective leadership, restored sufficient moral coherence to activate the divine promise encoded in this verse. The abundance is not the miracle — the moral restoration is. The abundance is merely its natural consequence.

The man who 'stands up and says: give me' and receives everything he can carry is a portrait of a civilization that has solved what modern economics calls the scarcity mindset — the anxiety-driven accumulation that produces hoarding, inequality, and the institutionalized violence of economic exclusion. Under Al-Mahdi's governance, abundance is real enough and trust sufficient enough that asking and receiving replaces the calculus of competitive extraction. This is the deepest meaning of 'filling the earth with justice': not merely eliminating visible oppression, but restoring the social ecology in which generosity becomes structurally rational.

> *For anyone who has experienced, even briefly, a community or institution in which genuine generosity was the default — where asking was not shameful and giving was not strategic — the description of Al-Mahdi's era resonates not as fantasy but as a recognition of what human social organization is capable of when its corrupting incentives are removed.*

VII. The Prayer Behind Al-Mahdi — Isa ibn Maryam's Arrival

Among the most structurally significant details in the Al-Mahdi narrations is one that is rarely given the analytical attention it deserves: when Isa ibn Maryam descends, he does not immediately assume leadership of the Muslim community. He prays behind Al-Mahdi. This single narrated detail carries profound implications for understanding the relationship between the two figures and the systemic logic of the entire End Times sequence.

> *Isa ibn Maryam will descend and their leader Al-Mahdi will say: Come lead us in prayer. But Isa will say: No — the honor of this Ummah is that some of them lead others.*

— Sahih Muslim, Hadith 156 — narrated by Jabir ibn Abdullah (RA)

The theological and systemic weight of Isa ibn Maryam praying behind Al-Mahdi cannot be overstated. Isa is, in Islamic belief, one of the five greatest prophets (Ulul Azm), born without a father, who performed miracles that no other prophet performed, and who will ultimately slay the Dajjal. That this figure defers to Al-Mahdi in the act of prayer is not a statement of relative superiority. It is a statement of sequential mission and institutional integrity.

Al-Mahdi's leadership is the established, legitimate, bay'ah-based authority of the Muslim community at that moment. Isa, by praying behind him, honors that institutional structure rather than superseding it. The message is systemic: legitimate authority, properly established through the bay'ah covenant, carries its own sanctity — one that even a prophet returning from the heavens respects and operates within rather than overriding. This is a statement about the integrity of institutional structures when they are genuinely grounded in divine sanction.

Furthermore, Isa's deferral signals the distinction between their missions. Al-Mahdi's mission is the restoration of justice within human civilizational structures. Isa's mission is the elimination of the Dajjal — the defeat of the deception system itself. These are sequential, complementary, non-competing missions. Al-Mahdi prepares the ground; Isa completes the correction. The prayer behind Al-Mahdi is the moment at which the handoff is signaled: the systemic restoration is sufficiently advanced for the final correction to begin.

> *For the believer who has ever wondered whether institutional structures matter when individual spiritual authority is present — this narration answers directly: they do. Isa ibn Maryam, with all his spiritual magnitude, honors the community's covenant structure. If that principle holds at the highest eschatological level, it holds everywhere.*

VIII. The Bay'ah in the Age of Broken Covenants

Modern political theory has, in the past century, systematically dismantled the conceptual architecture of the covenant as a binding moral and political act. The social contract tradition — from Locke to Rawls — attempted to ground political obligation in rational self-interest rather than moral and spiritual commitment. The result has been predictable: a political culture in which obligations are honored insofar as they serve self-interest and abandoned when they do not, and in which the concept of genuine, unconditional fidelity to a moral covenant is largely incomprehensible.

The bay'ah of Al-Mahdi, understood in its full theological and systemic depth, represents the polar opposite of this political culture. It is a covenant that neither party seeks for self-interest: Al-Mahdi accepts reluctantly, and the community pledges not to a charismatic individual but to a divine principle of justice that the individual embodies. The hand of Allah over all hands — yad Allah fawqa aydihim — is not rhetorical decoration. It is the structural element that makes the covenant binding in a way that no rational self-interest calculation can replicate.

THE BAY'AH AND THE MODERN CRISIS OF COVENANT

Modern political legitimacy: Grounded in electoral consent, legal procedure, rational self-interest

Result: Leaders honored when useful; discarded when inconvenient. Obligation = conditionality

Bay'ah legitimacy: Grounded in moral covenant, divine sanction, mutual obligation

Result: The leader accepts what they would refuse; the community commits beyond self-interest

"In an age where every institution is experienced as transactional, the

bay'ah of Al-Mahdi represents the return of covenant as the organizing principle of political life — the restoration of the binding moral agreement that makes genuine justice structurally possible."

The modern world has not outgrown the need for this. It has merely lost the vocabulary for it — and is paying the price of that loss in the very institutional failures the minor signs describe.

The comparison is not intended to suggest that modern democratic institutions are equivalent to the tyrants Al-Mahdi will displace. It is to identify the structural gap: between a political culture grounded in conditional self-interest and one grounded in unconditional moral covenant. The minor signs describe the consequences of that gap widening over generations. The bay'ah is the moment it closes.

> يَا أَيُّهَا الَّذِينَ آمَنُوا أَوْفُوا بِالْعُقُودِ
>
> *Ya ayyuha alladhina amanu awfu bil-'uqud*
>
> *"O you who have believed, fulfill all contracts."*
>
> **Surah Al-Ma'idah, 5:1**

The Quran's command to fulfill all contracts — awfu bil-'uqud — opens Surah Al-Ma'idah with a principle that classical scholars identify as one of the most comprehensive moral instructions in the entire Quran. Al-Tabari notes that al-'uqud encompasses covenants with Allah, covenants between people, and the obligations that flow from both. Al-Mahdi's bay'ah is the ultimate expression of awfu bil-'uqud at civilizational scale: a community fulfilling its covenant with justice, through a leader who fulfills his covenant with divine obligation, in a geography that fulfills its covenant with sacred history.

The Pivot of History

The bay'ah of Al-Mahdi is not the end of the story. It is, in the structural logic of the prophetic framework, the end of the beginning

— the moment at which the system's direction is definitively reversed and the trajectory toward justice becomes irreversible. What follows — the governance of Al-Mahdi, the descent of Isa ibn Maryam, the defeat of the Dajjal — all depend on this covenant being sealed in the precise manner the prophetic tradition describes.

Every element of the bay'ah carries diagnostic precision: the reluctance, the location, the chaos preceding it, the divine confirmation following it, the respect paid to it by the greatest figures in the End Times sequence. Together, these elements do not merely describe an event. They define the conditions under which genuine, durable, divinely-sanctioned justice becomes possible in a world that has exhausted every other option.

The world we live in — with its broken covenants, its transactional politics, its institutional emptiness — is not simply 'getting worse.' It is, in the prophetic framework, completing the conditions that make the bay'ah's necessity undeniable and its arrival inevitable. The harj wa marj is not a failure of human history. It is the labor pain before the birth of something the world has not seen since the early Muslim community and will not see again until Al-Mahdi stands between the Rukn and the Maqam, accepts what he did not seek, and changes the direction of everything.

> *For the reader who feels, in the chaos of the present moment, that nothing is steering — that systems are drifting without a corrective force, that institutions are hollow and authority is empty: the bay'ah is the prophetic answer. Not yet. But prepared for. And coming.*

The covenant is not signed by those who seek power.

It is pressed upon those who carry justice in their character — and can no longer refuse.

✦ ✦ ✦

Chapter Five: The Dajjal — The Architecture of Deception

continues on the following page...

CHAPTER FIVE

The Dajjal —
The Architecture of Deception

Of all the figures in Islamic eschatology, none has generated more popular fascination, more theological misreading, and more dangerous oversimplification than the Dajjal. He is routinely reduced to a one-eyed villain with supernatural powers — a figure drawn from the genre of cosmic horror, designed to terrify rather than to be understood. This reduction is itself a form of the very deception the Dajjal represents: the replacement of analytical clarity with emotional spectacle.

The Prophet Muhammad (peace be upon him) devoted more detailed, sustained, and specific prophetic description to the Dajjal than to any other single figure in eschatological narration. This is not because the Dajjal is the most powerful figure in the End Times sequence — he is not. He is killed by a single strike from Isa ibn Maryam. It is because he is the most dangerous. Not dangerous in the sense of military power, but dangerous in the precise sense that the Prophet Muhammad (peace be upon him) identified as the supreme threat to human moral and epistemic integrity: the manufacturing of a reality so convincingly false that the vast majority of people, including many who consider themselves believers, will accept it as true.

This chapter reads the Dajjal not as a horror story but as a systems analysis. It asks: what does the prophetic tradition actually authenticate about his identity, his powers, his methods, and his ultimate defeat? And then it asks the question that gives this chapter its modern urgency: in what sense has the world already begun building the Dajjal's infrastructure — not conspiratorially, but structurally — through the very technologies and institutions that now shape human reality?

> *For the person who has watched someone they loved be consumed by a false narrative — a political ideology, a manipulative relationship, a social media reality that bore no resemblance to actual life — and wondered how someone so intelligent could be so completely deceived: the Dajjal's mechanism is the answer, written at civilizational scale.*

I. What the Authenticated Narrations Actually Say

The hadith literature on the Dajjal is extensive, and not all of it meets the same standard of authentication. Before engaging the analytical framework, it is essential to establish what is rigorously authenticated and what belongs to the category of weaker or contextual narrations. The Prophet Muhammad (peace be upon him) warned so emphatically about the Dajjal that the authenticated narrations alone — in Sahih al-Bukhari, Sahih Muslim, and the major Sunan collections — provide a comprehensive and analytically sufficient portrait.

> *There is no prophet who was not sent to warn his people about the one-eyed liar. Truly he is one-eyed, and your Lord is not one-eyed. Written between his eyes is K-F-R (Kafir).*

— Sahih al-Bukhari, Hadith 7131; Sahih Muslim, Hadith 2933 — narrated by Ibn Umar (RA)

> *The Dajjal will emerge from a land in the East called Khurasan. He will be followed by peoples whose faces are like hammered shields.*

— Sunan al-Tirmidhi, Hadith 2237 — Hasan according to al-Tirmidhi

> *The Dajjal will come, and with him will be water and fire. What people see as water will be burning fire, and what they see as fire will be cold, sweet water. Whoever among you lives to see him, let him fall into that which appears to be fire, for it will be water.*

— Sahih al-Bukhari, Hadith 7130; Sahih Muslim, Hadith 2934 — Mutually authenticated

> *He will say to a Bedouin: What would you think if I resurrect your father and mother for you? He will say: Yes. Then two devils will appear to him in the form of his father and mother, saying: O my son, follow him.*

— Sahih Muslim, Hadith 2938 — narrated by Abu Umamah al-Bahili (RA)

These four narrations, drawn exclusively from the most rigorously authenticated sources, already establish the essential architecture of the Dajjal's deception: sensory inversion (fire appears as water), emotional manipulation through the simulation of the most intimate relationships (parents resurrected as demons), geographic origin, and the universal prophetic warning — the fact that every prophet warned about him signals that his threat is not confined to one era or one community. It is the terminal expression of a pattern of deception that runs through all of human history.

AUTHENTICATED DAJJAL ATTRIBUTES — CORE PROFILE

- Physical: One eye — right eye described as a floating grape (Bukhari 7407); left eye blind and protruding
- Written on forehead: K-F-R (Kafir) — readable by every believer regardless of literacy (Muslim 2934)
- Origin: Emerges from the East — from between Iraq and Syria according to various narrations
- Duration: 40 days — first day like a year, second like a month, third like a week, then normal days (Muslim 2937)
- Powers: Controls weather (apparently), commands apparent abundance and deprivation, simulates resurrection
- Weakness: Cannot enter Makkah or Madinah — angels guard their entrances (Bukhari 7124)
- Defeat: Killed by Isa ibn Maryam at the gate of Ludd (Lod) in present-day Israel (Muslim 2937)

II. The One Eye — Understanding the Symbol

The Dajjal's most prominent physical attribute — the single functioning eye — is among the most symbolically rich details in the entire prophetic tradition, and among the most analytically productive when read correctly. The Prophet Muhammad (peace be upon him) did not describe the Dajjal's single eye as merely a physical deformity. He contrasted it directly with the divine: 'Your Lord is not one-eyed.' This contrast is the key to the symbol's meaning.

The Arabic term used for the Dajjal's functioning eye — al-'ayn al-yumna, the right eye — is described in Sahih al-Bukhari as 'like a floating grape' (ka-annaha 'inabah ta'ifa): present, conspicuous, apparently functioning, but internally hollow and displaced. The left eye — normally the eye of depth perception and balance — is described as blind. Together, these attributes encode a precise epistemological portrait: a being with spectacular surface presentation and complete depth blindness. Everything the Dajjal shows you is vivid, compelling, and wrong at the level of reality.

> زُيِّنَ لِلنَّاسِ حُبُّ الشَّهَوَاتِ مِنَ النِّسَاءِ وَالْبَنِينَ
> وَالْقَنَاطِيرِ الْمُقَنطَرَةِ مِنَ الذَّهَبِ وَالْفِضَّةِ
>
> *Zuyyina lil-nasi hubbu al-shahawati mina al-nisa'i wal-banina wal-qanatiri al-muqantarati minal-dhahabi wal-fiddah*
>
> *"Beautified for people is the love of that which they desire — of women and sons, heaped-up sums of gold and silver..."*
>
> **Surah Aal-Imran, 3:14**

This verse describes the mechanism the Dajjal will weaponize at maximum scale: the beautification (tazyin) of desire — the rendering of what is harmful as irresistibly attractive. The Quran identifies tazyin as a fundamental feature of the nafs (ego-self) and of Shaytan's influence throughout human history. The Dajjal is the terminal, concentrated, maximally resourced expression of this mechanism. His single eye does not merely fail to see depth — it actively presents the surface as the totality of reality, making depth-blindness feel like complete vision.

The modern analytical parallel is unavoidable and must be engaged directly. The digital attention economy is structurally a one-eyed system: it is exquisitely optimized for surface engagement — visual impact, emotional arousal, social validation — and constitutionally blind to depth, context, consequence, and truth. Not by conspiracy, but by design: the metrics that drive its optimization (clicks, shares, watch-time, reactions) are all surface metrics. Depth cannot be measured by the algorithm, so depth is not what the algorithm rewards. The result is an information ecosystem that presents the most engaging falsehood as indistinguishable from verified reality — and calls the result 'content.'

> *For the parent who has watched their child spend hours in a world of algorithmically curated images and videos and wondered whether what they are seeing bears any relationship to reality — you are describing the one-eyed architecture in operation. Spectacular surface, no depth. The Dajjal's epistemological signature, rehearsed at scale before his arrival.*

III. Fire That Is Water — The Inversion of Reality

The most analytically significant of all the Dajjal's described attributes is neither his appearance nor his apparent supernatural powers. It is the specific inversion described in the mutually authenticated narration from Bukhari and Muslim: what appears to people as water is fire, and what appears as fire is water. The Prophet Muhammad's instruction — fall into the apparent fire, for it will be cool water — encodes the complete epistemological program needed to survive the Dajjal's era.

Consider what this instruction demands. It requires the individual to act against the testimony of their own senses — to override what appears vividly real in favor of what they have been told, on prophetic authority, is actually real. This is not merely a test of bravery. It is a test of epistemological loyalty: whether your ultimate allegiance is to your sensory experience of reality or to the divinely-transmitted framework for understanding reality correctly. The Dajjal's deception works precisely because it makes the false feel more real than the true.

> *Whoever reaches the time of the Dajjal among you, let him recite the opening verses of Surah Al-Kahf, for they are your protection from the Dajjal.*

— Sahih Muslim, Hadith 2937 — narrated by al-Nawwas ibn Sam'an (RA)

The prescription of Surah Al-Kahf as protection against the Dajjal has been analyzed by scholars across the centuries — Ibn Kathir, al-Nawawi, al-Qurtubi — and the scholarly consensus is that its protective power lies not in its recitation as a verbal charm but in its content as an epistemological training program. The four stories of Surah Al-Kahf — the People of the Cave, the man with two gardens, Musa and al-Khidr, and Dhul-Qarnayn — each address a different dimension of the Dajjal's deception: the test of faith against social pressure, the test of wealth and material reality, the test of knowledge and its limits, and the test of power and its proper use.

Surah Al-Kahf is, in this reading, the Quran's pre-emptive inoculation against the Dajjal's four primary attack vectors: social coercion, material seduction, epistemological confusion, and the corruption of power. Whoever internalizes its lessons has developed precisely the depth perception that the Dajjal's one-eyed reality cannot replicate.

> إِنَّا جَعَلْنَا مَا عَلَى الْأَرْضِ زِينَةً لَّهَا لِنَبْلُوَهُمْ أَيُّهُمْ أَحْسَنُ عَمَلًا
>
> *Inna ja'alna ma 'ala al-ardi zinatan laha linabluwahum ayyuhum ahsanu 'amala*
>
> *"Indeed, We have made that which is on the earth adornment for it that We may test them as to which of them is best in deed."*
>
> **Surah Al-Kahf, 18:7**

The opening of Surah Al-Kahf establishes the frame: the earth's adornment — its beauty, its material richness, its sensory appeal — is a test, not a reality. The Dajjal does not invent this test. He maximizes it. He concentrates the earth's seductive capacity into a single, mobile, humanoid system of temptation and deploys it at a moment when human civilization has, through the degradation described in the minor signs, reached maximum vulnerability to precisely this kind of material and sensory manipulation.

IV. The Dajjal's Powers — What Is Authentic and What Is Exaggerated

Popular eschatological literature has significantly embellished the Dajjal's powers beyond what the authenticated narrations actually describe. This embellishment is itself a form of the deception it purports to warn against: by making the Dajjal appear so overwhelmingly powerful that resistance seems futile, it produces precisely the paralysis that the prophetic tradition was designed to prevent. Establishing what the narrations actually authenticate — and what they do not — is therefore an act of intellectual and spiritual discipline.

POWER / ATTRIBUTE	AUTHENTICATION STATUS	ANALYTICAL SIGNIFICANCE
Apparent resurrection of the dead	Sahih Muslim 2938 — Authenticated. He will apparently kill and resurrect	Not true resurrection — the 'revival' is demonic simulation. Tests

	a man. One narration: 'he will kill him, then revive him, and nothing will happen after that.'	attachment to physical life over truth.
Control of rain and agriculture	Sahih Muslim 2937 — Authenticated. He will command sky to rain; wherever he goes, land flourishes. He will command it to withhold; land becomes barren.	The supreme material temptation: follow him and eat; reject him and starve. Tests whether material survival overrides moral conviction.
Speed of travel — moving like clouds driven by wind	Sahih Muslim 2937 — Authenticated. Will traverse the earth rapidly, spending 40 days total.	Compressed time + global reach: no geography of escape. Tests whether faith persists without physical distance as shelter.
Riding a huge donkey / special mount	Various narrations, varying authentication levels. Al-Albani grades some as Da'if.	Noted by scholars; details of the mount are less critical than the confirmed powers. Cited for context only.
Followed by seventy thousand Jews wearing crowns	Sahih Muslim 2944 — Authenticated. Specific description of his initial following.	Not a sectarian claim — a diagnostic detail about which communities will be most vulnerable to the specific deceptions he employs.
Cannot enter Makkah or Madinah	Sahih al-Bukhari 7124; Sahih Muslim 2942 — Dual authentication. Angels guard both cities.	The geography of refuge: these are not merely sacred cities but epistemological sanctuaries — spaces where the Dajjal's reality-distortion field cannot operate.

V. The Dajjal as Systemic Force — Beyond the Individual

The most consequential interpretive move in this chapter — and the one that gives it its analytical depth — is the recognition that the

Dajjal must be understood at two levels simultaneously: as a specific individual human being, and as a systemic force that predates and will culminate in that individual. The Prophet Muhammad (peace be upon him) himself authorized this dual reading.

> *Shall I not tell you something about the Dajjal that no prophet has told his people? He is one-eyed, and he will bring something like Paradise and Hell. What he calls Paradise will actually be Hell, and I warn you about him as Noah warned his people.*

— Sahih al-Bukhari, Hadith 3338; Sahih Muslim, Hadith 2936 — narrated by Ibn Umar (RA)

The phrase 'as Noah warned his people' is the key. Noah's warning was not about a single imminent event — it was about the sustained, civilizational pattern of rejection that had made destruction inevitable. The Dajjal is not a figure who appears suddenly from nowhere. He is the terminal concentration of a force — the force of organized deception, of manufactured false reality, of the systematic inversion of truth — that has been present throughout human history and reaches its maximum expression in his person at the End Times.

This dual reading — individual and systemic — has profound analytical implications. It means that the characteristics and methods of the Dajjal are already present and operational in the world, in pre-terminal form, before his physical emergence. The one-eyed reality, the fire-that-looks-like-water, the simulation of resurrection, the control of material abundance — all of these have structural analogues in existing systems of power, information, and social control. Identifying them is not fearmongering. It is the prophetic tradition's built-in diagnostic tool.

THE DAJJALIC SYSTEM — PRE-TERMINAL MANIFESTATIONS

INVERSION OF REALITY (Fire = Water):

Mass media ecosystems that present entertainment as information, engagement as truth, and viral falsehood as verified reality. The more emotionally compelling, the more likely to be believed regardless of factual content.

SIMULATION OF RESURRECTION (False Revival):

AI deepfakes that resurrect dead celebrities, simulate living public figures saying things they never said, and generate photorealistic false events. The 'revival' is technically compelling and morally hollow — exactly the authenticated description.

CONTROL OF MATERIAL ABUNDANCE (Rain and Famine):

Financial systems, trade sanctions, and algorithmic content distribution that reward compliance and punish dissent through material consequences. Follow the system's values and prosper; reject them and face economic and social exclusion.

COMPRESSED TIME AND GLOBAL REACH:

The 24-hour news-and-social-media cycle has achieved exactly the compressed temporal reality described in the minor signs. The Dajjal's 40-day global traversal, 'moving like clouds,' has a structural precursor in information that reaches every corner of the earth within hours.

NOTE: These are structural analogues — precursor conditions — not identifications of the Dajjal himself. The individual Dajjal is a specific future person. These systems are the infrastructure his era will fully inherit and maximize.

VI. Who Will Follow the Dajjal — and Why

Perhaps the most psychologically challenging element of the Dajjal narrations — and the one most consistently avoided in popular treatments — is the description of who will follow him. The Prophet Muhammad (peace be upon him) did not describe the Dajjal's followers as uniformly ignorant, wicked, or faithless. He described them in ways that are far more unsettling: they will be people who have been left epistemologically undefended by the very conditions the minor signs describe.

> *The Dajjal will be followed by seventy thousand Jews of Isfahan wearing Persian shawls. He will also be followed by many women, such that a man will have to tie up his*

> *mother, daughter, sister, and aunt out of fear that they will follow him.*

— **Sahih Muslim, Hadith 2944 — narrated by Anas ibn Malik (RA)**

The reference to women following the Dajjal in large numbers is not a statement about women's moral weakness. Classical scholars including Ibn Hajar and al-Nawawi consistently interpret this as a description of the population that has been left most epistemologically undefended by the social conditions of the era — most isolated, most emotionally vulnerable, most targeted by the Dajjal's specific methods of emotional manipulation and simulated care. It is a sociological observation about vulnerability, not a theological judgment about gender.

More broadly, the picture that emerges from the narrations is of a population that follows the Dajjal not because they are evil but because they are desperate. The conditions of harj wa marj — the material scarcity, the social isolation, the institutional betrayal, the exhaustion of false hope — have left vast numbers of people in precisely the state of vulnerability that the Dajjal is designed to exploit. He offers food to the hungry, rain to the thirsty land, apparent miracles to the spiritually starved. His followers are not choosing falsehood over truth in full knowledge of the alternative. They are choosing apparent relief over apparent abandonment.

> *For the reader who finds it difficult to understand how intelligent, decent people follow obviously destructive movements — whether political, religious, or ideological — the Dajjal's follower profile is not a mystery. It is the predictable outcome of extended epistemic deprivation. People do not follow falsehood because they prefer it. They follow it because it arrived when they were most in need, and truth was nowhere visible.*

WHO RESISTS THE DAJJAL	WHO FOLLOWS THE DAJJAL
Those whose faith is anchored in revealed knowledge, not sensory experience alone	Those whose reality is constructed primarily from sensory and material experience

Those who have cultivated depth perception — Surah Al-Kahf as epistemic training	Those left epistemologically undefended by the collapse of genuine scholarship (rafa' al-'ilm)
Those who recognize 'Kafir' written on his forehead — believers with active discernment	Those whose discernment has been dulled by sustained exposure to manufactured realities
Residents of Makkah and Madinah — the geography of refuge maintains epistemic clarity	Those in the Dajjal's physical presence — his reality-distortion field is proximity-dependent
Those who understood the minor signs and prepared intellectually and spiritually	Those who, exhausted by institutional betrayal, are desperate for any apparent solution

---

VII. The Geography of Refuge — Makkah, Madinah, and Al-Sham

The prophetic narrations identify specific geographies as sites of refuge during the Dajjal's era, and the analytical significance of these identifications extends beyond the merely logistical. The Dajjal cannot enter Makkah or Madinah — this is authenticated in both Bukhari and Muslim. The narrations also describe Al-Sham (the greater Syria region) as a place of gathering for the believing community and the site of significant eschatological events in the period surrounding the Dajjal's emergence.

> *The Dajjal will come to the outskirts of Madinah and it will shake three times. Every hypocrite, man and woman, will go out toward him; and every believer, man and woman, will remain.*

— Sahih al-Bukhari, Hadith 1881; Sahih Muslim, Hadith 2943 — narrated by Anas ibn Malik (RA)

This narration reveals a dimension of the Dajjal's function that is rarely analyzed: his arrival at Madinah does not merely test who follows him. It purges the community of its hypocrites. The shaking of Madinah — a city protected from his entry — still triggers the departure of those whose faith was always conditional and performed rather than genuine. The Dajjal, in this dimension, functions as the ultimate revealer of hidden states: his proximity strips away the social performance of faith and leaves only what is real.

The geography of Makkah and Madinah as epistemic sanctuaries is not merely a matter of physical protection from the Dajjal's presence. It is the protection offered by environments in which the framework of reality has been most consistently maintained — where the Quran is recited, the Sunnah is practiced, and the social environment continuously reinforces the depth-perceptual capacity that the Dajjal's one-eyed system cannot penetrate. The geography is a proxy for an epistemological ecology.

> يَا أَيُّهَا الَّذِينَ آمَنُوا اتَّقُوا اللَّهَ وَكُونُوا مَعَ الصَّادِقِينَ
>
> *Ya ayyuha alladhina amanu ittaqu Allaha wa kunu ma'a al-sadiqin*
>
> *"O you who have believed, fear Allah and be with the truthful."*
>
> **Surah Al-Tawbah, 9:119**

The Quranic command to be with the truthful (al-sadiqin) is, in the context of the Dajjal's era, the most practical protective instruction the tradition offers. The Dajjal's deception cannot operate in environments saturated with truthfulness — where people speak what they genuinely believe, where institutional structures are oriented toward accuracy rather than engagement, and where the social pressure runs toward honesty rather than performance. Building and inhabiting such environments is not merely a spiritual aspiration. It is the specific epistemological preparation that the prophetic tradition identifies as the antidote to the Dajjal's method.

VIII. The Dajjal and Al-Mahdi — Competing Realities

Within the systemic framework of this book, the relationship between Al-Mahdi and the Dajjal is not merely sequential — it is structural. Al-Mahdi represents the restoration of adl (justice) as the organizing principle of civilization. The Dajjal represents the maximization of zulm (oppression and distortion) through the industrialization of deception. They are not simply a hero and a villain. They are two competing operating systems for human civilization, running simultaneously during the same era of history.

Al-Mahdi's bay'ah establishes justice as the new attractor state — the organizing principle around which the corrected system begins to reorganize. The Dajjal's emergence represents the old system's final, maximum effort to reassert the attractor state of deception and oppression. Their coexistence in the same era is not a narrative oversight. It is the systemic logic of transition states: when a system is reorganizing, the old attractor and the new attractor compete for dominance, and the amplitude of their conflict is precisely proportional to the magnitude of the transition.

THE COMPETING OPERATING SYSTEMS

AL-MAHDI'S SYSTEM:

Adl (justice) as organizing principle | Amanah (trust) as social infrastructure | Authentic knowledge as epistemic foundation | Voluntary bay'ah as legitimate authority | Abundance through moral restoration

THE DAJJAL'S SYSTEM:

Zulm (distortion/oppression) as organizing principle | Manufactured fear and desire as control mechanisms | Sensory simulation as epistemological substitute | Material coercion (rain/famine) as compliance tool | Apparent abundance contingent on submission

THE DECISIVE DIFFERENCE:

Al-Mahdi's system requires the free, voluntary covenant of people who choose justice. The Dajjal's system requires the manufactured consent of people who cannot distinguish reality from its simulation. One builds on human dignity. The other exploits human vulnerability. This difference is precisely why the Dajjal is defeated not by military force but by truth — the lance of Isa ibn Maryam is merely the physical expression of a reality that has already been established.

The Most Warned-About Figure in Prophetic History

The Prophet Muhammad (peace be upon him) warned about the Dajjal more than about any other single threat in prophetic history. He instructed Muslims to seek refuge from the Dajjal's fitnah in every salah — in every prayer — as part of the final tashahhud. He prescribed Surah Al-Kahf as a weekly protective practice. He gave specific physical descriptions to enable recognition. He described the precise geography of refuge. He authenticated the specific methods of deception so that people could identify them.

All of this warning — accumulated, repeated, multi-dimensional — was not designed to produce fear. It was designed to produce preparation: the specific cognitive, spiritual, and epistemological preparation that the Dajjal's methods are designed to dismantle. A community that has genuinely absorbed the prophetic warning about the Dajjal is, by definition, a community that has developed depth perception — the capacity to distinguish reality from its simulation, truth from its counterfeit, genuine authority from its performance.

The Dajjal will fail not because he lacks power — he will have, in the moment of his maximum influence, more apparent power than any figure in human history. He will fail because the truth is not a competitor in a fair contest of appearances. It is the underlying operating system that all appearances, including the Dajjal's, must ultimately run on. When Isa ibn Maryam descends and the Dajjal flees and melts like salt in water — as the authenticated narrations describe — it will not be the defeat of a powerful figure by a more powerful one. It will be the dissolution of a sustained illusion in the presence of reality. The simulation cannot survive the return of what it was simulating.

> *For every generation that has lived under a system of manufactured reality — and every generation in some sense has — the defeat of the Dajjal is not just an eschatological event to await. It is the ultimate confirmation that reality outlasts its counterfeits. Always. The truth does not need to defeat the lie in fair competition. It only needs to remain itself.*

The Dajjal's power is not that he is stronger than the truth.

His power is that he arrives when people have forgotten what the truth feels like.

✦ ✦ ✦

Chapter Six: Isa ibn Maryam — The Final Correction

continues on the following page...

CHAPTER SIX
Isa ibn Maryam —
The Final Correction

Every system that has ever been corrupted carries within it the memory of what it was designed to be. The distortion is real, and its consequences are devastating — but underneath the distortion, the original architecture persists. Restoring a corrupted system does not require rebuilding from nothing. It requires the return of the original operating principles, applied with sufficient authority to override everything that has been layered over them. What the system needs is not innovation. It needs the return of truth.

In the prophetic architecture of the End Times, Isa ibn Maryam — Jesus, son of Mary, peace be upon him — is precisely this: the return of truth in its most concentrated, most unambiguous, most humanly embodied form. He does not arrive to found a new religion. He does not arrive to establish a new civilization. He arrives to complete what the system was always designed to produce — the total elimination of the Dajjal's deception and the confirmation of the divine order that Al-Mahdi's justice began to restore. He is the final correction. Not the beginning of something new, but the fulfillment of everything that was always true.

His descent is the most theologically rich, most cross-religiously significant, and most analytically consequential event in the entire End Times sequence. It is the moment at which the three Abrahamic traditions — Islam, Christianity, and Judaism — each encounter their own eschatological expectations meeting a single, specific, historically continuous figure. And it is the moment at which the systemic framework of this book reaches its logical conclusion: the corruption cycle is complete, the correction is complete, and the system can begin operating on the other side of its greatest crisis.

> *For the Christian reader who has spent a lifetime awaiting the Second Coming — and the Muslim reader who has studied the narrations of Isa's descent — this chapter is the place where two traditions, shaped by the same divine source, find themselves describing the same man, arriving at the same moment, for the same ultimate purpose. The differences in theology are real. The convergence in expectation is equally real.*

I. Who Is Isa ibn Maryam — The Islamic Portrait

Before engaging the eschatological role of Isa ibn Maryam, intellectual honesty demands establishing the Islamic portrait of who he is — precisely, theologically, and without conflating the Islamic understanding with its Christian or secular counterparts. The Quran speaks of Isa more than of any other prophet except Musa, and the portrait it presents is both exalted and carefully bounded.

> إِذْ قَالَتِ الْمَلَائِكَةُ يَا مَرْيَمُ إِنَّ اللَّهَ يُبَشِّرُكِ بِكَلِمَةٍ مِّنْهُ اسْمُهُ الْمَسِيحُ عِيسَى ابْنُ مَرْيَمَ وَجِيهًا فِي الدُّنْيَا وَالْآخِرَةِ
>
> *Idh qalati al-mala'ikatu ya Maryamu inna Allaha yubashshiruki bi-kalimatin minhu ismuhu al-Masihu 'Isa ibnu Maryama, wajihan fi al-dunya wal-akhirah*
>
> *"When the angels said, 'O Mary, indeed Allah gives you good tidings of a word from Him, whose name will be the Messiah, Jesus, the son of Mary — distinguished in this world and the Hereafter.'"*
>
> **Surah Aal-Imran, 3:45**

The title al-Masih — the Messiah — is preserved in the Islamic tradition with its full weight of eschatological significance. Isa is not merely a great prophet who has passed into history. He is, in the explicit Quranic framework, a figure of cosmic distinction in both this world and the next, whose story is unfinished. The Quran does not describe his death — it describes his raising:

> وَمَا قَتَلُوهُ وَمَا صَلَبُوهُ وَلَٰكِن شُبِّهَ لَهُمْ ۚ وَإِنَّ الَّذِينَ اخْتَلَفُوا فِيهِ لَفِي شَكٍّ مِّنْهُ ۚ بَل رَّفَعَهُ اللَّهُ إِلَيْهِ
>
> *Wa ma qataluhu wa ma salabuhu wa lakin shubbiha lahum... bal rafa'ahu Allahu ilayh*
>
> *"They did not kill him, nor did they crucify him; but it was made to appear so to them... Rather, Allah raised him to Himself."*
>
> **Surah An-Nisa, 4:157-158**

These two verses together establish the Quranic foundation for the entire eschatological role of Isa ibn Maryam: he was raised — rafa'ahu — not killed. He is therefore alive, in a state of divine preservation, and will return. His return is not a theological innovation grafted onto the tradition. It is the necessary completion of a narrative the Quran itself holds open. The descent of Isa ibn Maryam at the End Times is the Quran's own story arriving at its conclusion.

ISA IBN MARYAM — AUTHENTICATED ISLAMIC PROFILE

- Title: Al-Masih (the Messiah), Ruhullah (Spirit of Allah), Kalimatullah (Word of Allah)
- Status: One of the five greatest prophets — Ulul Azm — alongside Nuh, Ibrahim, Musa, Muhammad (pbuh)
- Current state: Raised alive to the heavens — not dead; awaiting the divine command to descend
- Descent location: Damascus — at the white minaret in the east of the city (Muslim 2937)
- Physical description at descent: Wearing two garments of light yellow (wardat), hair as if dripping water (Muslim 2937)
- First act: Prays behind Al-Mahdi — honors the established bay'ah community
- Primary mission: Kills the Dajjal at the gate of Ludd; breaks the cross; kills the pig; abolishes the jizyah
- Post-Dajjal era: Rules with justice for 40 years; then dies a natural death and is buried in Madinah

---

II. The Descent — What the Authenticated Narrations Describe

The descent of Isa ibn Maryam is among the most detailed and most rigorously authenticated events in the entire hadith literature on the End Times. The core narration — from Sahih Muslim — is a single extended report narrated by al-Nawwas ibn Sam'an that covers the Dajjal's emergence, Isa's descent, and the subsequent events in a connected sequence. It deserves to be quoted at length and analyzed with care.

> *Isa ibn Maryam will descend at the white minaret in the east of Damascus, wearing two garments lightly dyed with saffron, placing his hands on the wings of two angels. When he lowers his head, beads of perspiration will fall from it, and when he raises it, beads like pearls will scatter from it. Every disbeliever who smells the odor of his breath will die, and his breath will reach as far as he can see.*

— Sahih Muslim, Hadith 2937 — narrated by al-Nawwas ibn Sam'an (RA)

The physical description is precise and layered with meaning that classical commentators have analyzed with great care. The two light-yellow garments — wardat wa mihsama — signal purity and preparation for action, not ceremony. The hands on the wings of two angels signal the divine escort: Isa does not descend alone or under his own authority. He descends sent, accompanied, and commissioned. The breath that kills every disbeliever it reaches is the most analytically charged detail: it signals that his mere presence — the concentrated truth of his being, not any weapon — is what the Dajjal's deception system cannot survive.

The location — the white minaret in the east of Damascus — has generated centuries of scholarly discussion, and Ibn Kathir, in his Al-Nihayah, notes that the minaret of the Umayyad Mosque in Damascus is a candidate that has been discussed since the early centuries. Scholars differ on whether the narration refers to a specific existing structure or a structure that will be built, but they are unanimous on the city: Damascus, Al-Sham, the blessed land.

> وَإِن مِّنْ أَهْلِ الْكِتَابِ إِلَّا لَيُؤْمِنَنَّ بِهِ قَبْلَ مَوْتِهِ ۖ وَيَوْمَ الْقِيَامَةِ يَكُونُ عَلَيْهِمْ شَهِيدًا

Wa in min ahli al-kitabi illa layu'minanna bihi qabla mawtihi, wa yawma al-qiyamati yakunu 'alayhim shahida

"And there is none from the People of the Scripture but that he will surely believe in Jesus before his death. And on the Day of Resurrection he will be against them a witness."

Surah An-Nisa, 4:159

This verse is among the most theologically consequential in the Quran's treatment of Isa. The majority of classical commentators — Ibn Abbas, Ibn Kathir, al-Tabari, al-Qurtubi — understand 'before his death' as referring to Isa's death after his return, not the death of every individual from the People of the Scripture. The verse therefore encodes a Quranic promise: that when Isa descends in the End Times, every surviving person from the People of the Scripture who witnesses his return will believe in him — in his true identity, under his true mission. The cross will be broken not merely physically but epistemologically: the theological distortion of his identity will dissolve in the presence of the undistorted reality.

> *For the Christian who has spent a lifetime in faith, awaiting the return of Jesus — and who reads this chapter knowing that the Islamic tradition awaits the same figure — the convergence is not a theological threat. It is an invitation to sit with the profound question of what a tradition that has preserved his lineage and mission intact has to offer the tradition that bears his name.*

III. The Defeat of the Dajjal — Truth Dissolving Illusion

The manner in which Isa ibn Maryam defeats the Dajjal is among the most symbolically precise details in the entire End Times narrative, and it has been almost universally misread by popular treatments that focus on the physical act and miss its systemic meaning. The narrations describe Isa pursuing the Dajjal to the gate of Ludd — the city of Lod in present-day Israel — and killing him there. The weapon used is described in various narrations as a lance or spear.

> *The son of Mary will then kill the Dajjal at the gate of Ludd. Then a people whom Allah had protected will come to Isa ibn Maryam and he will wipe their faces and inform them of their ranks in Paradise.*

— Sahih Muslim, Hadith 2937 — narrated by al-Nawwas ibn Sam'an (RA)

> *The Dajjal will see Isa ibn Maryam and will begin to dissolve like salt dissolves in water. If Isa left him, he*

> *would dissolve completely on his own. But Allah will kill him at the hands of Isa, and he will show the people his blood on his lance.*
>
> **— Musnad Ahmad, Hadith 19499 — Hasan according to Shu'ayb al-Arnaut**

The image of the Dajjal dissolving like salt in water at the mere sight of Isa is the analytically decisive detail. The dissolution begins before the lance falls. The Dajjal does not die from a superior weapon — he begins dying from the presence of truth. The lance is the physical expression of an epistemological reality that has already rendered him irreversible in its outcome: in the presence of authentic, concentrated, unambiguous truth, the deception system cannot maintain its coherence. It dissolves. The killing is the physical completion of a dissolution that the spiritual reality has already begun.

This is the most important systemic insight in the entire End Times sequence: the Dajjal's power is not structural — it is dependent on the absence of its negation. His reality-distortion field can only operate in environments where genuine truth is sufficiently diluted. The moment truth arrives in concentrated, embodied, undeniable form — Isa ibn Maryam, descending from the heavens, sent by Allah — the deception system's preconditions for existence are removed. It does not lose a battle. It loses the ability to exist.

THE DEFEAT SEQUENCE — LUDD TO LIBERATION

① ISA DESCENDS AT DAMASCUS MINARET

Hands on angels' wings. Believers gather. The community of Al-Mahdi recognizes him immediately.

Sahih Muslim 2937

② PRAYER BEHIND AL-MAHDI

Isa defers to Al-Mahdi for the prayer. Institutional legitimacy of the bay'ah honored at the highest level.

Sahih Muslim 156

③ PURSUIT OF THE DAJJAL

Isa leads the believers in pursuit. The Dajjal flees as Isa approaches — the deception system detecting its negation.

Sahih Muslim 2937

④ **DAJJAL BEGINS DISSOLVING**

At the gate of Ludd, the Dajjal sees Isa and begins dissolving like salt in water — before the lance falls.

Musnad Ahmad 19499 — Hasan

⑤ **THE LANCE — DECEPTION ENDS**

Isa kills the Dajjal. Shows the people his blood on the lance. The physical completion of truth's victory.

Sahih Muslim 2937

⑥ **THE PEOPLE OF ALLAH EMERGE**

Those Allah had protected — believers who survived — come to Isa. He wipes their faces and tells them their stations in Paradise.

Sahih Muslim 2937

IV. Breaking the Cross — The Theological Completion

Among the specific acts attributed to Isa ibn Maryam after the Dajjal's defeat, the most theologically charged — and most frequently misunderstood — is his breaking of the cross (kasr al-salib). The narration is authenticated in Sahih al-Bukhari and has generated an enormous body of scholarly commentary across fourteen centuries.

> *By Him in Whose hands my soul is, surely Jesus son of Mary will descend among you and will judge mankind justly. He will break the cross, kill the pig, and abolish the jizyah. There will be an abundance of wealth, and nobody will accept charitable gifts.*

— Sahih al-Bukhari, Hadith 2222 — narrated by Abu Hurairah (RA)

The breaking of the cross has been interpreted in two complementary dimensions by classical scholarship. The first is theological: Isa's own act of breaking the cross is his personal, authoritative repudiation of the doctrine of crucifixion and the theological edifice that has been built upon it. He who was never crucified, who was raised alive by Allah, returns to personally dissolve the central symbol of the theological misreading of his identity and mission. This is not an act of hostility toward Christians — it is an act of love toward a tradition that distorted the reality of one of its most beloved figures.

The second dimension is systemic: the cross, in the context of the End Times, represents the organized religious authority that has been co-opted by the Dajjal's system. Ibn Kathir notes that by the time of Isa's descent, many religious institutions will have aligned with the Dajjal's reality — offering theological legitimacy to the deception system. The breaking of the cross is the dismantling of that co-option: the removal of the religious veneer from the deception architecture.

The killing of the pig (qatl al-khinzir) is the abolition of what has been made permissible by the distorted religious order — the normalization of what divine law prohibits, reframed as acceptable by those who shaped religion to serve the Dajjal's system. And the abolition of the jizyah signals the end of the political framework built on the distinction between protected and unprotected peoples — because in Isa's era, the distinction is resolved: all who remain will be under one truth, one law, one covenant.

> وَإِنَّهُ لَعِلْمٌ لِلسَّاعَةِ فَلَا تَمْتَرُنَّ بِهَا وَاتَّبِعُونِ ۚ هَٰذَا صِرَاطٌ مُسْتَقِيمٌ

Wa innahu la'ilmun lil-sa'ati fala tamtarunna biha wattabi'un, hadha siratun mustaqim

"And indeed, Jesus will be a sign of the Hour, so be not in doubt of it, and follow Me. This is a straight path."

Surah Az-Zukhruf, 43:61

The Quran's declaration that Isa is a sign of the Hour — 'ilmun lil-sa'ah — is one of the most direct Quranic confirmations of his eschatological role. Al-Tabari and the majority of classical commentators read this as referring specifically to his descent in the End Times as the definitive marker that the Hour is near. His return is not a peripheral eschatological detail. It is, by Quranic designation, the sign that the system has entered its final phase.

> *For the scholar who has spent years in the intersection of Islamic and Christian theology — navigating their*

> *convergences and their irreconcilable differences — this chapter does not ask for the dissolution of those differences. It asks for the recognition that the same figure, described across two traditions with different theological frames, is expected by both to return, to set right what has been distorted, and to complete what was always intended. That convergence is not small.*

V. Isa's Era — What Justice Looks Like After the Correction

Following the Dajjal's defeat, the authenticated narrations describe a period of Isa ibn Maryam's governance — typically narrated as forty years — that represents the fullest expression of divine justice that the earth has ever seen outside of prophetic governance. This era is not a supernatural paradise. It is a human civilization operating, for the first time since the early Muslim community, at the level of moral coherence that divine guidance was always designed to produce.

> *He will remain for forty years, then he will die and the Muslims will pray the funeral prayer over him.*

— Sunan Abu Dawood, Hadith 4324 — Hasan according to al-Albani

> *Isa son of Mary will descend and will kill the swine and abolish the jizyah. There will be no more enmity between people. Every harmful animal will be made harmless. The sky will send down its rain, the earth will bring out its blessings, and the children will play with lions.*

— Musnad Ahmad — reported through multiple chains; Ibn Kathir cites the collective narrations as strengthening each other

The description of children playing with lions is perhaps the most arresting image in the entire End Times corpus — and the most analytically layered. It is not merely a poetic description of peace. It is the description of the restoration of the natural order to its pre-fallen equilibrium: when human civilization is operating in genuine alignment with divine justice, the enmity between creation's elements — including the predator-prey relationships that characterize a world of scarcity and fear — is reorganized. This is the Quran's principle of fasad fil-ard (corruption in the earth) inverted: when the corruption is fully removed, the earth's own ecology responds.

ISA'S ERA — THE RESTORED SYSTEM

Duration: 40 years — sufficient for a complete civilizational generation to form under justice

Social ecology: No enmity between peoples. The social fragmentation described in the minor signs is fully healed.

Natural ecology: Rain abundant, earth productive, harmful animals rendered harmless. The ecological restoration that began under Al-Mahdi reaches completion.

Economic reality: Wealth so abundant that charity has no recipients. The material distortion of the minor signs is fully reversed.

Religious unity: The cross is broken; the theological distortions of Isa's identity are dissolved. All remaining believers worship under one truth.

Children and lions: The ultimate image of restored order — predation as a feature of a corrupted world, not of the original or final design.

Death of Isa: He dies a natural death after 40 years. Muslims pray over him. He is buried in Madinah, beside the Prophet Muhammad (pbuh).

VI. Comparative Lens — What Christianity and Judaism Expect

The eschatological return of Isa ibn Maryam is the point in the End Times narrative where the three Abrahamic traditions most directly intersect, and engaging that intersection with intellectual honesty requires acknowledging both the convergence and the irreducible theological differences. This book does not attempt to harmonize what cannot be harmonized. It attempts to map the landscape honestly.

ELEMENT	ISLAMIC EXPECTATION	CHRISTIAN EXPECTATION
Identity of the returning figure	Isa ibn Maryam — prophet, Masih, Ruhullah. Not divine. Not the son of God in the theological sense. A human being elevated and preserved by Allah.	Jesus Christ — divine Son of God, second person of the Trinity, returning in glory as the resurrected Lord and Judge.
Purpose of the return	Kill the Dajjal. Break the cross. Restore justice. Complete Al-Mahdi's mission. Live for 40 years, then die naturally.	Final judgment of the living and the dead. Establishment of the Kingdom of God. Eternal reign. No natural death in Christian eschatology.
What happens to his opponents	The Dajjal dissolves. His followers are defeated. Gog and Magog emerge subsequently and are destroyed by divine intervention.	The Antichrist is destroyed. Satan is bound for 1,000 years (Revelation). Final judgment separates the saved from the damned.
Nature of the era that follows	40 years of justice, abundance, natural harmony. Then Isa's death. Then subsequent signs, Gog and Magog, and eventually the Day of Judgment.	The Millennium (Revelation 20) — 1,000 years of Christ's reign, followed by the final rebellion, final judgment, and the New Creation.
The figure of the Dajjal / Antichrist	Al-Masih al-Dajjal — specifically named and described in hadith. One-eyed. Kafir written on forehead. Genuine individual. Duration 40 days.	The Antichrist — described in Revelation, Daniel, and the epistles of John. Features vary by tradition. Political, religious, and supernatural dimensions.

The convergences in this table are structural and significant. Both traditions expect: a supreme deceiver figure preceding the return; the return of the same specific person (Isa/Jesus); his defeat of that deceiver; and a subsequent era of unprecedented justice and peace. The theological differences around his nature — prophet versus divine person — are irreducible and must not be artificially dissolved. But the structural eschatological convergence is real, and it suggests that across the theological divide, both traditions are describing the same event from different angles of revelation.

The Jewish tradition's expectation adds a further layer. Classical Jewish eschatology awaits the Mashiach — a human king from the line of David who will rebuild the Temple, gather the exiles, and usher in the Messianic age. Isa ibn Maryam's return does not map directly onto this expectation in every particular. But the convergence in the structural logic — a world-historical correction executed through a specific individual who restores justice to a corrupted order — is present across all three traditions. The Quran's declaration that Isa 'will be a sign of the Hour' for all people, not only Muslims, is the most direct Quranic acknowledgment of his trans-traditional significance.

> *For the secular reader who finds the eschatological convergence of three major religious traditions around a single figure at a specific historical moment to be statistically remarkable — you are correct to notice. The question of what that convergence means is precisely the question that the End Times framework, read with analytical seriousness, invites every reader to sit with.*

VII. Isa's Role in the System — Completing What Al-Mahdi Began

The systemic framework of this book has traced a three-phase sequence across its chapters: Al-Mahdi as the initiation of the correction, the Dajjal as the maximum expression of the corruption that the correction must overcome, and Isa ibn Maryam as the completion of the correction. This sequence is not merely narrative. It is structural — each phase depends on the previous one, and each produces the conditions that make the next possible.

Al-Mahdi's bay'ah establishes justice as the new attractor state for civilization and demonstrates — through his governance — that a human community organized around adl and qist is viable. This is the necessary prerequisite: the Dajjal cannot be finally defeated while justice remains merely aspirational. It must be demonstrated as operational. Al-Mahdi's era is the proof of concept.

The Dajjal's emergence, following or overlapping with Al-Mahdi's era, represents the old attractor's final, maximum resistance: a force that concentrates all the deception, manipulation, and manufactured reality of human history into its most powerful expression. The fact that he emerges after Al-Mahdi's justice has been established is analytically significant: the Dajjal is not the cause of the world's corruption. He is its terminal amplification. His defeat is not the beginning of justice — it is the removal of the last obstacle to its completion.

Isa ibn Maryam's descent is therefore not a new beginning. It is a completion. The correction that Al-Mahdi initiated — the restoration of adl as civilization's operating principle — is finalized by the elimination of the deception system's architecture. With the Dajjal gone, the cross broken, the theological distortions of three millennia dissolved, and the natural and social ecologies restored, the system has achieved what the minor signs' accumulation was always pointing toward: not annihilation, but transformation.

THE THREE-PHASE SYSTEMIC COMPLETION

PHASE ONE — AL-MAHDI:

Initiates correction. Establishes adl. Proves justice is operational. Prepares the conditions for Isa's arrival. Prays in front; leads the community to the threshold.

PHASE TWO — THE DAJJAL:

Maximum resistance of the corruption system. Tests every human's epistemological loyalty. Is already dissolving before the lance falls — truth's mere presence is his undoing.

PHASE THREE — ISA IBN MARYAM:

Completes the correction. Eliminates the deception architecture. Breaks the religious distortion of his own identity. Governs 40 years in the fullest justice the earth has ever seen. Then dies — naturally, humanly, in Madinah.

THE SYSTEM PRINCIPLE:

The correction does not require destroying humanity. It requires removing everything that prevented humanity from being what it was always designed to be. Al-Mahdi starts the removal. Isa completes it. The system then runs, for 40 years, on its original design.

VIII. The Death of Isa — Why He Must Die

The detail that Isa ibn Maryam, after his return, will live for forty years and then die a natural death — and be buried in Madinah beside the Prophet Muhammad (peace be upon him) — is one of the most humanly significant details in the entire End Times narration. And it is one of the least discussed.

His death is not a failure. It is not the end of his mission's effects. It is the completion of his humanity — the final affirmation that he was, is, and will always have been a human being: mortal, temporary, a servant of Allah rather than an equivalent of Allah. Every theological tradition that elevated him beyond humanity has, through that elevation, done him a disservice. His natural death after forty years of governance is the prophetic tradition's most definitive theological statement about his nature: he is the greatest of servants. Not the master.

> *The Prophet Muhammad (pbuh) said: I am the closest of all people to Jesus son of Mary in this world and the Hereafter. The prophets are paternal brothers — their mothers are different but their religion is one.*

— Sahih al-Bukhari, Hadith 3443 — narrated by Abu Hurairah (RA)

This hadith places Isa within the prophetic brotherhood — the same family of divine guidance, the same essential mission of truth, differentiated only in their specific roles and communities. The Prophet Muhammad's closeness to Isa is not merely personal affection. It is the recognition that their missions are the most tightly coupled in all of prophetic history: Muhammad's mission established the final revelation; Isa's return will fulfill the final application of that revelation. The burial of Isa in Madinah — beside the Prophet — is the physical expression of that eternal coupling.

> *For the reader who has encountered Jesus in their own tradition — whether as Lord, as prophet, as teacher, or as historical figure — the portrait of a man who lived a perfect mission, was raised rather than killed, and returns to complete what he began, then dies peacefully among those who love him and is buried in the holiest city of the final revelation: there is a beauty in this portrait that transcends the theological dispute around it. It is the portrait of service fulfilled.*

The Final Correction and What It Means

Isa ibn Maryam's descent is not the end of the world. It is the end of the world as it has been corrupted. What follows — the era of his governance, the death of Gog and Magog through subsequent divine intervention, the gradual approach of the Day of Judgment — belongs to the chapters that follow this one. But his descent marks the completion of the systemic correction that this book has been tracing from the accumulation of the minor signs through Al-Mahdi's bay'ah through the Dajjal's deception.

The three-part correction — Al-Mahdi restoring justice, Isa completing truth's victory, the system reorganizing around both — is the prophetic tradition's answer to the question that haunts every civilization in decline: is correction possible, or does entropy always win? The answer the tradition gives is precise. Entropy wins every battle in which the correction is only human. It loses the war when the correction is divinely commissioned, humanly executed, and sequentially structured in the exact manner the prophetic tradition describes.

The world after Isa's return is not perfect in the sense of being free from all difficulty. Gog and Magog emerge after his era. The Day of Judgment remains. The system does not arrive at utopia — it arrives at its designed state: a human civilization, finally operating on the principles it was always designed to embody, for as long as it has before the final accounting begins. That is not a small thing. That is everything the minor signs were lamenting the loss of.

> *For every generation that lived through the accumulation of signs and wondered whether the correction would arrive in time — Isa ibn Maryam's return is the prophetic tradition's answer. Not in time by your calendar. In time by the divine architecture. The system was always going to produce this moment. You were living in its preparation.*

He does not return to judge. He returns to complete.
The correction was always going to require a truth that no deception could dissolve — and no death could silence.

✦ ✦ ✦

Chapter Seven: Gog and Magog — The Final Entropy

continues on the following page...

CHAPTER SEVEN
Gog and Magog —
The Final Entropy

Every system that achieves a stable, just equilibrium carries within it a latent vulnerability: the possibility that forces external to its corrected order — forces that were contained, not eliminated —

will eventually surge through whatever boundary contained them. Al-Mahdi restores justice. Isa ibn Maryam defeats the Dajjal and governs in truth. The system achieves, for forty years, the closest approximation to its intended design that post-Adamic history has ever produced. And then Gog and Magog are released.

This sequence is not a narrative failure. It is the final proof of a theological principle that runs through the entire Quran: that the earth's test is never permanently resolved by human governance alone, however righteous. Even the most just civilizational order that has ever existed — Isa's forty-year governance — cannot permanently contain the forces of entropy that are built into the structure of a world designed for testing. Gog and Magog are not the failure of the correction. They are its final examination: the ultimate stress test of a civilization that has been restored to its highest functioning, now faced with an overflow that no human force can resist.

Their emergence — and their destruction by divine intervention alone, without any human military response — draws the clearest possible line between what human agency can achieve and what only divine agency can resolve. Al-Mahdi's justice was human agency at its best, divinely facilitated. Isa's governance was prophetic authority at its highest, divinely commissioned. Gog and Magog's destruction belongs to neither category. It is pure divine intervention: worms in their necks, overnight, without a single arrow fired. The message is precise: there is a category of terminal entropy that lies beyond the corrective capacity of even the most exalted human or prophetic governance. Only Allah resolves it.

> *For the reader who has ever wondered why history's greatest moral recoveries — the best leaders, the most just periods — always seem to be followed by collapse: the Gog and Magog narrative is the prophetic tradition's most honest answer. The correction was always temporary. The test was never designed to end with human success. It was designed to end with divine resolution.*

I. Who Are Gog and Magog — Establishing the Evidence

Yajuj and Ma'juj — Gog and Magog — appear in both the Quran and the authenticated hadith tradition, making them among the most multiply-sourced figures in Islamic eschatology. They appear in the narrative of Dhul-Qarnayn in Surah Al-Kahf, in Surah Al-Anbiya, and in numerous narrations in Sahih al-Bukhari and Sahih Muslim. Understanding who they are requires engaging all these sources systematically, while distinguishing between what is definitively authenticated and what belongs to the category of scholarly interpretation or da'if narration.

> حَتَّىٰ إِذَا فُتِحَتْ يَأْجُوجُ وَمَأْجُوجُ وَهُم مِّن كُلِّ حَدَبٍ
> يَنسِلُونَ
>
> *Hatta idha futihat Yajuju wa Majuju wa hum min kulli hadabin yansilun*
>
> *"Until when Gog and Magog are let loose and they swarm from every elevated place."*
>
> **Surah Al-Anbiya, 21:96**

The Quranic description is economical and precise: they are released — futihat, passive voice, by divine command — and they swarm from every elevated place. The verb yansilun — to pour forth rapidly, like a rushing stream — conveys both the speed and the overwhelming numerical scale of their emergence. This is not a military force in any conventional sense. It is a flood — a human flood of such magnitude that the earth itself cannot contain it.

> قَالَ هَٰذَا رَحْمَةٌ مِّن رَّبِّي ۖ فَإِذَا جَاءَ وَعْدُ رَبِّي جَعَلَهُ
> دَكَّاءَ ۖ وَكَانَ وَعْدُ رَبِّي حَقًّا
>
> *Qala hadha rahmatun min Rabbi, fa-idha ja'a wa'du Rabbi ja'alahu dakka'a, wa kana wa'du Rabbi haqqa*
>
> *"He said: This is a mercy from my Lord; but when the promise of my Lord comes, He will make it level — and the promise of my Lord is ever True."*
>
> **Surah Al-Kahf, 18:98**

Dhul-Qarnayn's statement upon completing the barrier against Gog and Magog is deeply instructive. He does not claim the barrier is permanent. He explicitly acknowledges that when the promise of his

Lord arrives, it will be leveled — dakkaa. The barrier between Gog and Magog and the rest of the world was always a temporary mercy, not a permanent solution. The divine promise of their release was built into the structure of their containment from the moment the barrier was raised.

GOG AND MAGOG — AUTHENTICATED PROFILE

- Quranic mentions: Surah Al-Kahf 18:94-99 (barrier of Dhul-Qarnayn); Surah Al-Anbiya 21:96 (their release)
- Hadith sources: Sahih al-Bukhari 3346, 7135; Sahih Muslim 2937, 2881 — multiply authenticated
- Identity: Human beings — a specific people, descendants of Adam (Muslim 2781 confirms they are human)
- Current state: Contained behind a barrier, attempting to break through daily — authenticated in Bukhari and Muslim
- Release timing: After Isa ibn Maryam's governance begins — following the Dajjal's defeat
- Scale: Their numbers are so vast that the sea of Tiberias (Sea of Galilee) will be drunk dry by their passage
- Destruction: By worms (al-na'ghaf) sent into their necks — overnight, without human military action
- Aftermath: Birds carry their bodies; earth is cleansed by rain; civilization must rebuild

---

II. The Barrier of Dhul-Qarnayn — A Temporary Mercy

The narrative context for Gog and Magog in the Quran is the story of Dhul-Qarnayn — the great traveler and ruler whose identity scholars have debated for centuries. Ibn Kathir, al-Tabari, and al-Qurtubi all engage this question extensively, and the scholarly disagreement on whether Dhul-Qarnayn was Alexander the Great, Cyrus of Persia, or another figure has never been definitively resolved. What is beyond scholarly dispute is the Quranic account itself: a people, dwelling between two mountains, appealing to a powerful ruler to build a barrier against the destructive raids of Gog and Magog.

> قَالُوا يَا ذَا الْقَرْنَيْنِ إِنَّ يَأْجُوجَ وَمَأْجُوجَ مُفْسِدُونَ فِي الْأَرْضِ فَهَلْ نَجْعَلُ لَكَ خَرْجًا عَلَىٰ أَنْ تَجْعَلَ بَيْنَنَا وَبَيْنَهُمْ سَدًّا
>
> *Qalu ya Dhal-Qarnayni inna Yajuja wa Majuja mufsiduna fi al-ardi fa-hal naj'alu laka khraj'an 'ala an taj'ala baynana wa baynahum sadda*
>
> *"They said: O Dhul-Qarnayn, indeed Gog and Magog are corrupters in the land. So may we assign for you an expenditure that you might make between us and them a barrier?"*
>
> **Surah Al-Kahf, 18:94**

The phrase mufsiduna fil-ard — corrupters in the land — is the Quran's diagnostic label for Gog and Magog's essential character. It is the same phrase used in the Quran to describe the fundamental mode of those who oppose divine order: fasad, corruption, the disruption of the natural and moral equilibrium that Allah's design maintains. Gog and Magog are not described as merely militarily powerful. They are described as ontologically disruptive — beings whose presence in the world, uncontained, produces corruption at a scale that overwhelms every human capacity for resistance.

The barrier — al-sadd — built by Dhul-Qarnayn with iron and copper was the divine mercy that delayed this confrontation. The communities protected behind it could develop, civilizations could rise and fall, prophets could come and go, and the correction cycle of the End Times could play out — all because this particular flood of entropy was temporarily held back. The narrations in Sahih al-Bukhari describe Gog and Magog digging at the barrier each day until they have almost broken through, then returning the next day to find it restored. This daily cycle of almost-breakthrough and divine restoration is precisely the systemic condition of a world that is perpetually on the edge of terminal entropy — held back only by a mercy that has an expiration date.

> *For the historian who has studied the cycles of civilizational rise and fall and wondered what force keeps producing the same pattern of expansion, peak, and*

> *collapse — the Gog and Magog framework offers an answer that no secular historical model produces: that the deepest driver of civilizational entropy is not internal corruption alone, but a pressure at the boundary of the corrected order that the corrected order cannot itself permanently resolve.*

III. The Release — What the Authenticated Narrations Describe

The narrations describing Gog and Magog's release and rampage form one of the most vivid and most multiply-authenticated clusters in the entire End Times hadith corpus. The core account appears in the long hadith of al-Nawwas ibn Sam'an in Sahih Muslim — the same narration that describes Isa's descent and the Dajjal's defeat — making the sequential connection between these events explicit and anchored in a single, unbroken chain.

> *Allah will reveal to Isa: I have brought forth servants of Mine whom no one will have the power to fight. Take my servants safely to the mountain of Tur. Then Allah will send Gog and Magog, and they will swarm down from every slope. The first of them will pass by the Sea of Tiberias and drink it dry; the last of them will pass by and say: There was once water here.*

— Sahih Muslim, Hadith 2937 — narrated by al-Nawwas ibn Sam'an (RA)

Three systemic observations from this narration demand careful attention. First: the divine command to Isa to take the believers to the mountain of Tur — not to fight, but to retreat. This is among the most counter-intuitive instructions in the entire prophetic narrative: the greatest human governance of all time, led by the returned prophet who just defeated the Dajjal, is instructed not to engage Gog and Magog militarily. The retreat is not cowardice. It is the recognition of a categorical distinction: this is not a challenge that human or prophetic authority is designed to resolve.

Second: the Sea of Tiberias drunk dry by their passage. The Sea of Galilee — one of the most significant freshwater bodies in the

Middle East — is consumed not as an act of deliberate destruction but as an incidental consequence of their sheer number. This is not a military campaign. It is a natural disaster in human form: overwhelming, indiscriminate, and resistant to conventional response. The system cannot fight a flood with weapons.

Third: the last of them saying 'there was once water here.' This detail — the trailing edge of the horde arriving after the water is already gone — encodes the narration's most analytically significant datum: their numbers are so vast that the gap between their first and last member is measured in the time it takes a sea to be drunk dry. This is the description of a force whose scale is categorically beyond any human military calculation.

THE GOG AND MAGOG SEQUENCE

① DIVINE COMMAND TO ISA — RETREAT TO TUR

Allah commands Isa to withdraw the believers to Mount Tur. No military engagement ordered. A categorical boundary is drawn.

Sahih Muslim 2937

② GOG AND MAGOG RELEASED FROM THE BARRIER

The barrier leveled overnight. They pour forth from every elevated place — yansilun. The flood begins.

Surah Al-Anbiya 21:96; Surah Al-Kahf 18:98

③ SEA OF TIBERIAS CONSUMED

The first wave drinks the Sea of Galilee dry. The trailing edge finds no water. Scale beyond all military calculation.

Sahih Muslim 2937

④ ARROWS FIRED INTO THE SKY

They fire arrows into the sky — an act of arrogance against Heaven itself. The arrows return bloodied. They believe they have killed the inhabitants of the sky.

Sahih Muslim 2937; Ibn Majah 4079 — Da'if element noted; core event in Muslim

⑤ ISA AND BELIEVERS UNDER SIEGE ON TUR

Isa and the believers are surrounded and unable to descend. They make du'a to Allah. Human agency has reached its absolute limit.

Sahih Muslim 2937

⑥ **DIVINE DESTRUCTION — WORMS IN THEIR NECKS**
Allah sends al-na'ghaf — a worm — into the necks of Gog and Magog. They die overnight, every one of them. Not one human hand raised.
Sahih Muslim 2937; Sunan Ibn Majah 4079 — Hasan

⑦ **EARTH CLEANSED — RAIN AND REBUILDING**
Birds carry away the bodies. Allah sends rain. The earth brings forth its fruit. Civilization begins the long process of genuine restoration.
Sahih Muslim 2937

IV. The Arrows Into the Sky — The Theology of Arrogance

Among the most theologically significant details in the Gog and Magog narrative is the account of their firing arrows into the sky — and the arrows returning to them apparently bloodied. This detail, narrated in Sahih Muslim's extended account, is among the most analytically layered in the entire End Times corpus, and has generated careful commentary from scholars including Ibn Kathir and al-Nawawi.

> *They will send their arrows into the sky, and the arrows will come back to them stained with blood. And they will say: We have killed the people of the sky. Then Allah will destroy them.*
>
> — **Sahih Muslim, Hadith 2937 — the core element; extended detail in Sunan Ibn Majah with varying chain strength**

Ibn Kathir's commentary in Al-Nihayah is instructive: the arrows returning bloodied is understood as either a trial — a false sign permitted by Allah to test the arrogance of Gog and Magog further — or as a matter involving birds struck in the sky whose blood stained the returning arrows. What is unanimous in the scholarly tradition is the interpretation of this act: it represents the supreme expression of the arrogance that characterizes Gog and Magog's essence. Having consumed the earth's water, having overwhelmed the earth's forces, they turn their aggression toward Heaven itself.

In systemic terms, this is the terminal expression of a principle that runs through the entire End Times sequence: that entropy, left unchecked, does not merely consume the horizontal plane of human civilization. It eventually turns vertical — directed against the divine order itself. The Dajjal's deception was the horizontal expression: manufacturing false reality for human consumption. Gog and Magog's arrows are the vertical expression: direct aggression against the source of reality. It is the logical endpoint of a civilization that has progressively replaced divine authority with human autonomy, and human autonomy with raw power.

> أَلَمْ تَرَ أَنَّ اللَّهَ يَسْجُدُ لَهُ مَن فِي السَّمَاوَاتِ وَمَن فِي الْأَرْضِ

Alam tara anna Allaha yasjudu lahu man fi al-samawati wa man fi al-ard

"Do you not see that to Allah prostrate whoever is in the heavens and whoever is on the earth?"

Surah Al-Hajj, 22:18

This verse — establishing the universal prostration of everything in the heavens and earth before Allah — is the Quranic reality that Gog and Magog's arrows are aimed against. Their act of firing into the sky is the ultimate declaration that they recognize no authority above them. It is the metaphysical culmination of fasad fil-ard: not merely corruption of the earth, but the attempted assertion of sovereignty over the divine. Their destruction follows immediately in the narration. The arrows aimed at Heaven return to earth. The worm in the neck is the divine response to the arrow aimed at the divine.

> *For the reader familiar with modern civilization's trajectory — the displacement of divine authority by human self-sufficiency, the progressive assertion that no reference point outside human consensus is legitimate — Gog and Magog's arrows are not an alien image. They are the logical endpoint of the trajectory, rendered in prophetic language. The question is not whether the arrows will be fired. It is whether we recognize the arc of their flight before they reach us.*

V. The Divine Destruction — Why No Human Hand Is Raised

The manner of Gog and Magog's destruction is the single most analytically significant detail in their entire narration. Not a military campaign. Not a supernatural weapon wielded by Isa ibn Maryam. Not a collective du'a that produces divine thunder or flood. A worm. Sent into their necks. Overnight. Every one of them dead by morning. The believers descend from Mount Tur to find a landscape carpeted with bodies and no enemy remaining.

> *Then Isa and his companions will supplicate to Allah, and Allah will send upon them insects that will attack their necks — and in the morning they will all be found dead, like the death of a single soul. Then Isa and his companions will descend to the earth and they will not find a spot on earth that is not filled with the stench and decaying remains of Gog and Magog.*

— Sahih Muslim, Hadith 2937 — narrated by al-Nawwas ibn Sam'an (RA)

The phrase 'like the death of a single soul' — ka-nafsin wahidatin — is extraordinary. An army of hundreds of millions, perhaps billions, dying simultaneously, overnight, as if they were one person. This image has a precise systemic meaning: Gog and Magog, despite their overwhelming numbers, were never genuinely individuated. They were always a single force — entropy in mass human form — and they die as a single force. The worm that ends them is not fighting individuals. It is terminating a system.

Why a worm? The scholars — Ibn Kathir, al-Nawawi, al-Qurtubi — consistently note that the choice of instrument is the theological statement. The most overwhelming force the earth has ever produced — a force that drank a sea, that fired arrows at Heaven, that besieged the returned prophet himself — is not defeated by an army or a cataclysm. It is defeated by the smallest possible instrument of divine will. The gap between Gog and Magog's scale and the instrument of their destruction is the measurement of divine sovereignty. Allah does not need to match the scale of the threat with the scale of the response. He needs only to will it.

> إِنَّمَا أَمْرُهُ إِذَا أَرَادَ شَيْئًا أَن يَقُولَ لَهُ كُن فَيَكُونُ

Innama amruhu idha arada shay'an an yaqula lahu kun fa-yakun

"His command is only when He intends a thing that He says to it: Be — and it is."

Surah Ya-Sin, 36:82

The worm in the neck of Gog and Magog is the narrated, physical, historical expression of kun fa-yakun — the divine command that requires nothing between intention and outcome. No logistics. No coalition. No strategy. Be — and it is. Their death is the final demonstration, in the clearest possible terms, of the principle that has governed the entire End Times sequence: that the ultimate correction of the human system is not achievable by human agency alone, however exalted. It requires the direct exercise of divine will. Al-Mahdi showed what human agency at its best can achieve. Isa showed what prophetic authority can complete. The worm shows what only Allah can resolve.

VI. The Scholarly Debates — Identity, Geography, and Scale

The question of Gog and Magog's identity has generated more scholarly debate, across more traditions and more centuries, than almost any other eschatological question. The Islamic scholarly tradition has engaged it with characteristic rigor — and characteristic diversity of opinion. Presenting the landscape of these debates is essential for intellectual honesty, even where definitive resolution is impossible.

QUESTION	SCHOLARLY POSITIONS	EVIDENTIAL BASIS
Are they human beings?	Yes — unanimous. Sahih Muslim 2781 explicitly states they are children of Adam. Any narration suggesting otherwise is rejected by scholars.	Sahih Muslim 2781 — explicit. Surah Al-Kahf 18:94 — the people of that land speak to Dhul-Qarnayn about them as a neighboring human group.
Who are they	Classical opinion: Turkic or	No authenticated hadith

historically?	Mongolic peoples (Ibn Kathir, al-Tabari). Modern opinion: humanity's unredeemable corruptive impulse. Ibn Khaldun: unknowable without direct prophetic specification.	specifies their ethnic identity with the precision required for certainty. Scholars differ. The Quran does not name their ethnicity.
Where is the barrier?	Various locations proposed: the Caucasus mountains, central Asia, northern China. No scholarly consensus. The barrier's current location is unknown and may be divinely concealed.	Al-Kahf 18:93 describes a place between two mountains (bayna al-saddayn). No hadith specifies its geographic coordinates with authenticated precision.
Are they being released gradually or all at once?	All at once — the barrier is leveled by divine command at a specific moment. The narration of daily digging and nightly restoration in Bukhari 3346 describes their pre-release condition, not a gradual release.	Sahih al-Bukhari 3346; Sahih Muslim 2881 — the barrier restoration narration; Surah Al-Anbiya 21:96 — released at once.
Are Gog and Magog already among us?	Scholars differ. Some note that the barrier's current status is unknown and that the 'daily digging' narration may be metaphorical. Others hold the barrier is physical and extant. No consensus.	Sahih al-Bukhari 7135 — the Prophet saw a hole in the barrier in a vision. Does not confirm it has been breached.

The honest scholarly position is that the specific identity and current location of Gog and Magog cannot be determined from the authenticated textual evidence alone. What can be determined is their essential character — mufsiduna fil-ard — and their eschatological role: the final, unsuppressible surge of entropy that arrives after the greatest human correction and can only be resolved by direct divine intervention. This functional description is what carries analytical weight, regardless of which specific people or force it will ultimately correspond to.

> *For the reader uncomfortable with the scholarly uncertainty — who wants the map to be complete and the identities definitive — this chapter offers something more*

valuable than false certainty: the recognition that the tradition's honesty about what it does not know is itself a mark of its intellectual integrity. The prophetic tradition is specific where specificity is given and honest where it is not.

VII. Gog and Magog in Comparative Tradition

Gog and Magog appear not only in the Islamic tradition but in the Hebrew Bible, the New Testament Book of Revelation, and in various ancient Near Eastern traditions — making them one of the most cross-traditional eschatological figures in world religious literature. The comparative analysis is analytically productive precisely because the convergences and divergences illuminate what each tradition's specific understanding adds to the overall picture.

ISLAMIC TRADITION	BIBLICAL / CHRISTIAN TRADITION
Human beings — children of Adam, containing behind a barrier built by Dhul-Qarnayn (Al-Kahf 18:94-98)	Gog from the land of Magog — Ezekiel 38-39: a ruler (Gog) who leads a coalition against Israel
Released after Isa's return — post-Dajjal, during Isa's governance era	Revelation 20:7-8: Released after the Millennium — Satan deceives the nations after 1,000 years of Christ's reign
Destroyed by worm sent into necks — pure divine intervention; no human military response	Ezekiel 39: Destroyed by fire, brimstone, earthquake, pestilence — divine intervention but through natural forces
Scale: Drink the Sea of Galilee dry; number beyond military calculation	Revelation 20:8: 'Like the sand of the seashore' — similar emphasis on uncountable numbers
Aftermath: Birds carry bodies; rain cleanses; earth bears fruit; civilization rebuilds	Ezekiel 39:4, 17-20: Birds and beasts consume the fallen; 7 months to bury the dead; 7 years burning weapons

The structural convergences across these traditions are striking: an overwhelming force of unprecedented scale, released after a period of divine governance or prophetic correction, destroyed entirely by divine action rather than human military resistance, followed by a cleansing of the earth. The theological frameworks differ — Islamic tradition locates the event within a precise sequential structure; the Ezekiel narrative is geographically and politically specific in ways that require separate scholarly analysis; Revelation's Millennium context differs from Islam's forty-year governance timeline. But the essential shape — final entropy, divine termination, earth's restoration — is present across traditions in a way that invites serious comparative engagement rather than dismissal.

VIII. The Final Entropy — What Gog and Magog Mean for the System

The systemic framework of this book has traced the End Times sequence as a three-phase correction: Al-Mahdi initiating justice, Isa completing the correction, the system restored to its intended design. Gog and Magog represent the fourth element in this framework — one that is not part of the correction but its ultimate stress test: the discovery that even a fully corrected system, operating at its highest moral capacity under prophetic governance, cannot permanently contain the entropy that is built into the structure of a finite world.

This is the theological statement that Gog and Magog make about the nature of justice in a world of testing. Justice — adl — is achievable. Al-Mahdi achieves it. Isa sustains it. But justice in this world is always achievable against a background of contained entropy, not eliminated entropy. The barrier held Gog and Magog at bay during the entire human story. The moment it is lifted — by divine command, at the appointed time — the corrected system discovers that its correction was always provisional. The test was never designed to conclude with human success. It was designed to conclude with the revelation that human success, however real and however righteous, cannot be the final word.

THE FINAL ENTROPY — SYSTEMIC ANALYSIS

WHAT GOG AND MAGOG REPRESENT IN THE SYSTEM:

They are not a military enemy — they are contained entropy finally released. No army, no correction, no prophetic authority can hold them back once the divine permission for their release arrives.

THE LIMIT OF HUMAN AGENCY (including prophetic):

Al-Mahdi = human agency at its divinely-facilitated best. Isa = prophetic authority at its highest commission. Both retreat to Mount Tur. Neither fights. The limit of all human and prophetic capacity is clearly drawn.

THE INSTRUMENT OF RESOLUTION:

A worm. The smallest possible agent of divine will applied to the largest possible force of human entropy. This gap is the measurement of divine sovereignty — and the final rebuttal to every ideology that grounds human hope in human capacity alone.

THE THEOLOGICAL CONCLUSION:

The world was never designed to be permanently correctable by its own internal mechanisms. The correction of Al-Mahdi and Isa was real, righteous, and historically unprecedented. It was also always temporary. The permanent resolution awaits not the end of Gog and Magog but the end of the world as a testing ground — the Day of Judgment, when the test concludes and the accounting begins.

The aftermath of Gog and Magog's destruction is described in the narrations with careful detail: the believers descend from Tur, the birds carry away the bodies, Allah sends rain, the earth brings forth its blessings, and a pomegranate is so large that a group of people can eat from it and shelter in its skin. This is not mere poetic decoration. It is the Quranic principle of Surah Al-A'raf 7:96 — blessings from heaven and earth for communities that live in alignment with divine guidance — operating in its final terrestrial expression. The earth, cleansed of its greatest corruption, produces at its maximum capacity for the last time.

> وَأَخْرَجَتِ الْأَرْضُ أَثْقَالَهَا
>
> *Wa akhrajati al-ardu athqalaha*
>
> *"And the earth has brought forth its burdens."*

Surah Az-Zalzalah, 99:2

This verse — from the short, thunderous Surah Az-Zalzalah, describing the earth's final convulsion before the Day of Judgment — captures in four Arabic words what the post-Gog-and-Magog period represents: the earth giving up everything it has been holding. Its blessings, its fruit, its capacity for abundance — all released in the final chapter of its terrestrial life. The system has been corrected, tested to its absolute limit by Gog and Magog, and is now producing its last gift before the accounting begins.

> *For every generation that worked toward justice and wondered whether it would last — whether the correction would hold, whether the next generation would maintain what this one built — Gog and Magog are the honest answer: it will not last forever. And that is not a failure. The test was never about permanence. It was about whether you chose justice when you had the choice.*

The Meaning of Final Entropy

Gog and Magog occupy a precise and irreplaceable position in the End Times architecture. They are not a narrative epilogue to the main story of Al-Mahdi, the Dajjal, and Isa. They are the final theological statement that the main story was always making: that the correction of a world under test is real, achievable, and divinely guaranteed — and that the world under test is, by design, always finite. The correction does not produce eternity. It produces the precondition for the final accounting.

What comes after Gog and Magog's destruction — the remaining major signs, the three sinkings of the earth, the smoke (dukhan), the emergence of the Beast (Dabbah), the rising of the sun from the West, the gentle wind that takes the souls of all believers, and finally the trumpet of the Day of Judgment — belongs to the chapters that follow. But the meaning of Gog and Magog is already complete: the world has been tested to its maximum, corrected to its maximum, and tested beyond its corrective capacity. What remains is not more testing. It is the resolution of all the testing that has ever occurred.

The prophetic tradition does not present this as tragedy. It presents it as design. The world was always going to arrive at this point. The barrier was always going to be lifted. The worm was always going to be sent. The earth was always going to give up its burdens. The question was never whether — it was always who would use the time between now and then to choose justice, to recognize the signs, to maintain what is true in the face of what is overwhelming. That question was always the point.

> *For the reader who reaches this point in the book and feels the weight of the full picture — the minor signs accumulated, the bay'ah sealed, the Dajjal defeated, Isa governing, and then Gog and Magog released — the weight is appropriate. This is not a comfortable framework. It is an honest one. And an honest framework is the only foundation on which genuine courage is possible.*

The greatest force of entropy in human history
is defeated not by the greatest army,
but by the smallest expression of divine will.

✦ ✦ ✦

Chapter Eight: The Remaining Major Signs — The World's Final Hours

continues on the following page...

CHAPTER EIGHT

The Remaining Major Signs — The World's Final Hours

A symphony does not end when its most dramatic movement concludes. After the climax, after the tension of the development section has resolved and the recapitulation has restored the original themes, there is a coda — a closing passage that does not introduce new material but draws together every thread, confirms every resolution, and brings the work to the silence that makes it complete. The coda is not a lesser part of the symphony. It is the part that tells you the symphony is over.

The remaining major signs of the Hour function precisely as this coda. Al-Mahdi restored justice. The Dajjal was defeated. Isa ibn Maryam governed in truth and died. Gog and Magog were released and destroyed by divine will. What follows — the three sinkings of the earth, the smoke that envelops the world, the emergence of the Beast, the rising of the sun from the West, the gentle wind that carries away every believing soul, and finally the trumpet blast that ends the world — are not new themes. They are the confirmation that every theme has been heard, every test completed, and the symphony of human existence is arriving at its final, irreversible silence.

This chapter does not merely catalogue these signs. It reads them as a system — identifying the logic that connects them, the theological principles they encode, and the precise sequence in which the authenticated narrations place them. And it asks the question that this entire book has been building toward: what does this complete picture mean for how a person lives in the period before the coda begins?

> *For the person who reads eschatology not as an intellectual exercise but as a framework for living — who wants to know not just what will happen but what it means for how to spend the hours between now and then — this chapter is the book's most personal address. The signs are almost all in place. The coda is close. The question is what you do with the remaining measures.*

I. The Complete Sequence — The Ten Major Signs

The hadith tradition identifies ten major signs of the Hour as a group, most comprehensively in a single authenticated narration from Sahih Muslim. While the minor signs are numerous and diffuse — accumulating across decades and centuries — the major signs are discrete, irreversible, and sequential. Each one, once it occurs, cannot be undone. Together they form the closing chapter of the human story, from the first definitive bifurcation point (Al-Mahdi's bay'ah) to the final trumpet blast.

> *The Hour will not be established until you have seen ten signs: the Smoke, the Dajjal, the Beast, the rising of the sun from the West, the descent of Isa ibn Maryam, Gog and Magog, three sinkings of the earth — one in the East, one in the West, and one in the Arabian Peninsula — and a fire that will drive the people to their place of gathering.*
>
> **— Sahih Muslim, Hadith 2901 — narrated by Hudhayfah ibn Usayd al-Ghifari (RA)**

This narration from Sahih Muslim — one of the most comprehensive single-hadith summaries of the major signs — gives us the authoritative list. Al-Mahdi is not named here but is confirmed by the broader hadith corpus as the initiating major sign preceding the Dajjal's emergence. The sequence is not rigidly linear in all cases — scholars including Ibn Kathir and al-Qurtubi note that some signs may overlap in time — but the general trajectory is clear: from the initiation of the correction (Al-Mahdi) through its completion (Isa, Gog and Magog) to the final closing of the world's account (the remaining signs below).

THE TEN MAJOR SIGNS — MASTER SEQUENCE

① **AL-MAHDI** — *First Major Sign*

Bay'ah between Rukn and Maqam. Justice (adl) established. System correction begins. Army sent against him swallowed by the earth.

Abu Dawood 4286 — Sahih | Sahih Muslim 2882

② **THE DAJJAL** — *Peak Deception*
Emerges from the East. Controls apparent weather and abundance. One-eyed. Kafir on forehead. 40 days. Fire appears as water.
Sahih Bukhari 7131 | Sahih Muslim 2933-2937

③ **ISA IBN MARYAM** — *Final Correction*
Descends at Damascus minaret. Prays behind Al-Mahdi. Defeats Dajjal at Ludd. Breaks cross. Governs 40 years. Dies in Madinah.
Sahih Muslim 2937 | Bukhari 2222

④ **GOG AND MAGOG** — *Final Entropy*
Released after Isa's governance. Drink the Sea of Galilee. Besiege Tur. Destroyed by worm overnight. Earth cleansed by rain.
Sahih Muslim 2937 | Surah Al-Anbiya 21:96

⑤ **THREE SINKINGS OF THE EARTH (Khusuf)** — *Geographic Ruptures*
East, West, Arabian Peninsula. Massive geographic collapses swallowing cities and peoples. Irreversible physical disruption of the earth's surface.
Sahih Muslim 2901 | Sunan Abu Dawood 4311

⑥ **THE SMOKE (Dukhan)** — *Atmospheric Affliction*
A smoke that fills the earth. Causes painful suffering for disbelievers; affects believers like a mild cold. Covers the world for 40 days.
Sahih Muslim 2901 | Surah Ad-Dukhan 44:10-11

⑦ **THE BEAST (Dabbat al-Ard)** — *Final Witness*
Emerges from the earth. Speaks to people. Marks believers and disbelievers. The final earthly messenger — not for guidance, for demarcation.
Sahih Muslim 2901 | Surah An-Naml 27:82

⑧ **RISING OF THE SUN FROM THE WEST** — *Door of Repentance Closes*
The sun rises from its setting point. The door of repentance (tawbah) closes permanently. No new faith or repentance accepted after this point.
Sahih Bukhari 4635 | Sahih Muslim 2941

⑨ **THE GENTLE WIND (Rih Tayyibah)** — *Believers Taken*
A gentle, cool wind takes the soul of every person with even a mustard seed's weight of faith. Only the worst of people remain alive.
Sahih Muslim 2940

⑩ **THE FIRE — DRIVING TO AL-MAHSHAR** — *Final Gathering*
A fire emerges from Yemen, driving all remaining people toward the place of gathering (al-Mahshar) in Syria. The trumpet sounds. The world ends.
Sahih Muslim 2901 | Sahih Bukhari 3329

II. The Three Sinkings — Khusuf and the Earth's Rupture

The three sinkings of the earth — khusuf — are among the least analyzed yet most geologically arresting of all the major signs. Unlike the personal and moral dimensions of the Dajjal or the epic scale of Gog and Magog, the khusuf are physical, geographic, and irreversible: massive collapses of the earth's surface in three specific regions, swallowing whatever — and whoever — is upon them. They represent the earth itself participating in the closing of the world's account.

> *There will be three sinkings of the earth: one in the East, one in the West, and one in the Arabian Peninsula. After that, a fire will emerge from Yemen that will drive the people to their place of gathering.*

— Sahih Muslim, Hadith 2901 — narrated by Hudhayfah ibn Usayd al-Ghifari (RA)

> *When the booty is distributed unequally, trust is betrayed, and the sinkings of the earth occur — watch for the wind, the red dust storm, and the khusuf — then the matter has appeared.*

— Sunan Abu Dawood, Hadith 4311 — Hasan according to al-Albani

The geographic distribution of the three sinkings — East, West, Arabian Peninsula — is analytically significant. Together, they encompass the three axes of human civilizational concentration: the East (historically Asia and the civilizations of the Indus, Ganges, Yellow River, and beyond), the West (historically Europe and the Atlantic world), and the Arabian Peninsula (the spiritual center of the Islamic world, where the Ka'bah stands). No region of the earth's major civilizations is excluded from this final geographic rupture.

Classical scholars including Ibn Kathir and al-Qurtubi interpret the khusuf as divine punctuation: the earth, which has served as the arena of the human test, begins physically dismantling that arena. The sinkings are not punishment in the traditional sense — by this point in the sequence, the major moral sorting has largely occurred. They are the literal dissolution of the physical stage on which the drama of human existence was performed. The set is being struck. The performance is ending.

The modern geological resonance is unavoidable but must be held carefully. Earthquake science, plate tectonics, and the known seismic instability of regions in each of these three axes — the Pacific Ring of Fire, the Eurasian Seismic Belt, and the Arabian tectonic plate — provide a natural-order framework within which such events could occur. This does not reduce them to mere geology. It suggests that the divine often acts through the natural order it created, and that the distinction between divine intervention and natural process is not the distinction most people assume.

> *For the geologist or earth scientist reading this — who has spent a career understanding the tectonic forces that make such events not merely possible but inevitable on geological timescales — the prophetic framework does not contradict your science. It gives it a meaning your instruments cannot measure.*

III. Al-Dukhan — The Smoke That Fills the Earth

The Dukhan — the smoke — is explicitly named in the Quran as a sign of the Hour, making it one of the most directly Quranic of all the major signs. Surah Ad-Dukhan — named for this very sign — opens with one of the most atmospherically charged passages in the entire Quran, and its relevance to the End Times sequence is both direct and analytically rich.

> فَارْتَقِبْ يَوْمَ تَأْتِي السَّمَاءُ بِدُخَانٍ مُّبِينٍ ﴿١٠﴾ يَغْشَى النَّاسَ ۖ هَٰذَا عَذَابٌ أَلِيمٌ

Fartaqib yawma ta'ti al-sama'u bi-dukhanin mubin, yaghsha al-nasa, hadha 'adhabun alim

"Then watch for the day when the sky will bring a visible smoke, covering the people — this is a painful punishment."

Surah Ad-Dukhan, 44:10-11

The description of the Dukhan in the Quran is precise in its effect: it covers people — yaghsha al-nasa — and it constitutes a painful punishment for those who denied the truth. The authenticated hadith tradition adds a layer of systemic differentiation that gives the sign its full analytical significance: the Dukhan affects believers and disbelievers differently.

> *The Dukhan will emerge and will seize the disbeliever, and it will affect him like a severe fever; as for the believer, it will affect him like a cold.*
>
> **— Sunan al-Tirmidhi, Hadith 3254 — narrated by Abu Hurairah (RA); scholars differ on its grading; al-Albani classifies it Sahih**

The differentiated effect of the Dukhan — severe for the disbeliever, mild for the believer — is the sign's theological core. It is not a uniform natural disaster. It is a discriminating punishment: the same atmospheric phenomenon producing radically different experiences depending on the spiritual state of the one who encounters it. This principle — that the same divine action produces different effects in different moral states — runs through the Quran's entire framework of signs and tests.

THE DUKHAN — SYSTEMIC ANALYSIS

QURANIC DESIGNATION: Named in Surah Ad-Dukhan 44:10-11 — one of the few major signs explicitly named in the Quran itself, not only in hadith.

NATURE: A visible, atmospheric smoke — dukhan mubeen (manifest/visible smoke) — that covers all people globally for a period narrated as approximately 40 days.

DIFFERENTIATED EFFECT: For the disbeliever — agonizing, like severe fever. For the believer — mild, like a cold. The same phenomenon; two entirely different experiences. This is the sign's theological signature: the end of undifferentiated human experience.

SCHOLARLY DEBATE: Ibn Masood held the Dukhan already occurred at Makkah during a famine in the early Muslim period. The majority of scholars — including Ibn Kathir and al-Nawawi — hold this was a partial or earlier manifestation, and the major Dukhan as named in the hadith of the ten signs is a future event of far greater scale.

SYSTEMIC POSITION: Occurs alongside or near the other terminal signs. By this point, the door of repentance is approaching its closure. The Dukhan is among the final opportunities for the remaining disbelievers to respond — and many, the narrations suggest, will ask for relief but not offer genuine repentance.

IV. Dabbat al-Ard — The Beast of the Earth

The Dabbah — the Beast that emerges from the earth — is among the most enigmatic of all the major signs, generating the widest scholarly diversity of interpretation and the most careful analytical restraint from classical scholars who recognized the limits of what the authenticated evidence allows. Unlike the Dajjal or Isa ibn Maryam, whose descriptions are extensive across multiple narrations, the Dabbah's nature and appearance are described in the Quran in a single verse and elaborated only partially in the hadith literature.

> وَإِذَا وَقَعَ الْقَوْلُ عَلَيْهِمْ أَخْرَجْنَا لَهُمْ دَابَّةً مِّنَ الْأَرْضِ
> تُكَلِّمُهُمْ أَنَّ النَّاسَ كَانُوا بِآيَاتِنَا لَا يُوقِنُونَ

Wa idha waqa'a al-qawlu 'alayhim akhrajna lahum dabbatan mina al-ardi tukallimuhum anna al-nasa kanu bi-ayatina la yuqinun

"And when the word of punishment comes down upon them, We will bring forth for them a creature from the earth speaking to them, because mankind was not certain about Our signs."

Surah An-Naml, 27:82

Three elements of this verse carry decisive analytical weight. First: the Dabbah speaks — tukallimuhum. It communicates with people. This is not a dumb animal unleashed upon humanity. It is a creature with communicative capacity, delivering a specific message. Second: its emergence is linked to the coming down of 'the word' — al-qawl — upon the people. This is the language the Quran uses for the final divine verdict: the point at which judgment is no longer pending but active. Third: the message it delivers — that people were not certain about Allah's signs — is a retrospective verdict, not a call to repentance. By the time the Dabbah speaks, the window for responding to signs has closed.

> *The Beast will emerge, and it will have with it the staff of Musa and the ring of Sulayman. It will mark the face of the believer with the ring, so that it shines, and it will mark the nose of the disbeliever with the staff, so that it darkens. Until a person sits at a table with his family, and it will be known — this one is a believer, and this one is a disbeliever.*
>
> **— Sunan Abu Dawood, Hadith 4322 — narrated by Abu Hurairah (RA); Hasan according to al-Albani**

The marking of believers and disbelievers — with instruments associated with Musa and Sulayman, two of the greatest prophets — encodes the Dabbah's precise function. It is not an agent of destruction. It is an agent of final demarcation: the permanent, publicly visible differentiation of faith from its absence. By the time the Dabbah marks the faces, the moral sorting that the entire sequence of major signs was designed to produce is complete. Every person who remains carries a mark that reflects the reality of their spiritual state — visible to all, permanent, and no longer subject to human self-presentation or social performance.

The Dabbah is, in this systemic reading, the end of ambiguity. The minor signs allowed people to see the warning signs and choose their response. The major signs — the Dajjal, Isa's return, Gog and Magog — provided the ultimate tests of epistemological loyalty and moral conviction. The Dabbah's marking is the moment when the results of those tests are made externally and permanently visible. The examination is over. The marks are posted.

> *For the person who has spent their life navigating between the private reality of their faith and the social performance of it — who has felt the gap between what they genuinely believe and what they publicly present — the Dabbah's marking is not a threat. It is a relief. The age of performance is over. What is real is finally simply real.*

V. The Rising of the Sun from the West — The Door Closes

Of all the ten major signs, the rising of the sun from the West is the most cosmologically arresting — and the one whose prophetic significance is most precisely and unanimously understood by classical scholarship. It is the sign after which repentance (tawbah) is no longer accepted and new faith is no longer credited. It is, in the most literal sense, the closing of the door through which human spiritual accountability flows.

> *The Hour will not be established until the sun rises from the West. When it rises and the people see it, they will all believe — but that will be the time when 'its faith will not benefit a soul that did not believe before or earn good through its faith.'*

— Sahih al-Bukhari, Hadith 4635; Sahih Muslim, Hadith 157 — narrated by Abu Hurairah (RA)

The hadith quotes directly from the Quran — Surah Al-An'am 6:158 — making this one of the most explicitly Quran-anchored hadith in the entire corpus. The principle it encodes is the most theologically precise in the entire End Times sequence: the rising of the sun from the West is not primarily a cosmological event, though it is that. It is an epistemological event: the moment when the evidence for divine reality becomes so undeniable — so viscerally, visually, inescapably obvious — that belief is no longer an act of faith. It is simply a response to overwhelming evidence.

> هَلْ يَنظُرُونَ إِلَّا أَن تَأْتِيَهُمُ الْمَلَائِكَةُ أَوْ يَأْتِيَ رَبُّكَ أَوْ
> يَأْتِيَ بَعْضُ آيَاتِ رَبِّكَ ۗ يَوْمَ يَأْتِي بَعْضُ آيَاتِ رَبِّكَ لَا
> يَنفَعُ نَفْسًا إِيمَانُهَا

Hal yanthuruna illa an ta'tiyahumu al-mala'ikatu aw ya'tiya Rabbuka aw ya'tiya ba'du ayati Rabbika, yawma ya'ti ba'du ayati Rabbika la yanfa'u nafsan imanuha

"Are they waiting for the angels to come, or for your Lord, or for some of your Lord's signs to come? The day when some of your Lord's signs do come, no soul's faith will benefit it if it did not believe before."

Surah Al-An'am, 6:158

This verse encodes the principle of faith's irreducible voluntariness: belief that is compelled by undeniable evidence is not the belief that was being tested. The test was always whether a person would believe in the unseen — bi al-ghayb — when the evidence was present but not overwhelming, when doubt was possible and faith was a choice. The rising of the sun from the West eliminates choice. Therefore, it eliminates the possibility of the kind of faith that the test was designed to reward.

The systemic implication is profound: the entire history of divine signs — from the miracles of the prophets to the minor signs to the major signs — was a graduated programme of evidence, calibrated to allow genuine faith to remain a choice. The sun from the West is the point at which the graduation programme ends. Beyond this, there is no more test. There is only accounting.

BEFORE THE SUN RISES FROM WEST	AFTER THE SUN RISES FROM WEST
Faith is a choice — bi al-ghayb (belief in the unseen)	Faith becomes involuntary response to undeniable evidence
Repentance (tawbah) accepted — the door is open	Tawbah no longer accepted — Surah Al-An'am 6:158 in force
Good deeds credited to one's account of faith	No new spiritual credits possible — the ledger is closed
Human beings can still change their spiritual trajectory	All trajectories are fixed — what was chosen is what stands
The test is ongoing — every moment carries moral weight	The test is over — what remains is the preparation for accounting

VI. Al-Rih al-Tayyibah — The Wind That Takes the Believers

Among all the remaining major signs, the most humanly tender — and the most analytically significant in terms of what it reveals about divine mercy — is the Rih Tayyibah: the gentle, sweet wind that takes the soul of every person who carries even a mustard seed's weight of genuine faith. It is the moment at which Allah removes His most beloved servants from the world before its final, ugliest chapter.

> *Allah will send a wind like the blowing of a pleasant breeze — it will come from the direction of Yemen. It will not leave a single person in whose heart there is a mustard seed's weight of good, but it will take his soul. Then the worst of people will remain, and upon them the Hour will be established.*
>
> **— Sahih Muslim, Hadith 2940 — narrated by Abdullah ibn Amr (RA)**

The gentleness of the wind — tayyibah, literally pure, pleasant, agreeable — is the theological statement. The death of the believers at this stage of history is not a punishment. It is a mercy. Allah removes every person who carries genuine faith before the world enters its final, most degraded state — the state in which the trumpet will sound and the worst of people will be those who witness the Day of Judgment while still alive.

The standard of removal is significant: 'a mustard seed's weight of good.' This is not the standard of the righteous scholar or the pious worshipper. It is the minimum threshold of genuine moral good — the irreducible core of whatever authentic goodness remains in a person. The wind does not discriminate between the deeply righteous and the marginally good. It takes everyone in whom genuine good persists, regardless of degree. This is the mercy principle at its most expansive: even the barely-faithful are protected from the world's final degradation.

> *For the person who worries whether their faith is sufficient — who measures themselves against the scholar's depth or the saint's devotion and finds themselves inadequate — the gentle wind is the most personally reassuring detail in the entire End Times narration. A mustard seed. That is the threshold. Allah's mercy in this final mercy is calibrated to include, not to exclude.*

What remains after the wind's passage is described in Sahih Muslim with a precision that is both sociological and tragic: the worst of people. Those in whom not even a mustard seed of genuine good remained. They are not merely irreligious — they are the terminal product of the moral inversion described in the minor signs, the generation that the Dajjal's reality-distortion field and Gog and Magog's overwhelming entropy has finally produced: human beings from whom the last traces of moral orientation have been stripped. Upon them the Hour will be established.

VII. The Fire, the Gathering, and the Trumpet

The final major signs form a closing sequence of three movements: the fire that drives the remaining people toward the place of gathering, the gathering itself at al-Mahshar, and the trumpet blast that ends the world as it has been known and initiates the Day of Judgment. Each is authenticated in the major hadith collections and carries a precise systemic function in the architecture of the End.

> *The last of the signs will be a fire that will drive people from the East to the West. It will spend the night with them wherever they spend the night and the day with them wherever they spend the day.*

— Sahih al-Bukhari, Hadith 3329 — narrated by Abu Hurairah (RA)

The fire is not a punishment in the conventional sense — by this point in the sequence, all genuine believers have been taken by the gentle wind. What remains is the population in whom no genuine faith persists. The fire drives them — not consuming them, but herding them — toward the place of gathering in al-Sham (Syria), where the accounting will begin. It is the final mobilization of the remaining human population toward the single location at which divine justice will be dispensed.

The detail that the fire 'spends the night wherever they spend the night' — that it accompanies rather than destroys — is the sign's distinguishing feature. It is not executing judgment. Judgment belongs to the Day itself. The fire is performing a logistical function in the most cosmic sense: gathering what remains of humanity to the place where the final accounting requires them to be. It is patient, persistent, and all-encompassing. No one escapes. No one is left behind.

> *The trumpet will be blown, and there will be no one between the heavens and the earth who will not fall unconscious — except those whom Allah wills. Then it will be blown a second time, and they will be standing, looking on.*

— Sahih Muslim, Hadith 2955 — narrated by Abu Hurairah (RA)

The trumpet — al-Sur — is blown twice. The first blast produces universal unconsciousness or death: everything between heaven and earth collapses. The second blast produces the resurrection: all of humanity standing, looking on, ready for the accounting. Between these two blasts — in the narrations, a period whose duration belongs to divine knowledge alone — the world as it has been known does not exist. What exists is the silence between the last note of the symphony and the moment the conductor's hands fall still.

> وَنُفِخَ فِي الصُّورِ فَصَعِقَ مَن فِي السَّمَاوَاتِ وَمَن فِي الْأَرْضِ إِلَّا مَن شَاءَ اللَّهُ ثُمَّ نُفِخَ فِيهِ أُخْرَىٰ فَإِذَا هُمْ قِيَامٌ يَنظُرُونَ

Wa nufikha fi al-suri fa-sa'iqa man fi al-samawati wa man fi al-ardi illa man sha'a Allah, thumma nufikha fihi ukhra fa-idha hum qiyamun yanthuruna

"And the trumpet will be blown, and whoever is in the heavens and whoever is on the earth will fall dead, except whom Allah wills. Then it will be blown again, and at once they will be standing, looking on."

Surah Az-Zumar, 39:68

VIII. The System Complete — What the Full Sequence Means

The ten major signs, read as a complete system rather than a list of isolated events, encode the most comprehensive moral and theological statement in the entire Islamic eschatological framework. They are not a series of disasters visited upon an unsuspecting world. They are the final, structured dissolution of the testing environment

— each sign performing a specific function in the orderly conclusion of the human examination.

Al-Mahdi and Isa's era represent the testing environment at its highest functioning: justice operative, truth visible, the system demonstrating what it was always designed to produce when human agency aligns with divine guidance. The Dajjal and Gog and Magog represent the testing environment at its most extreme stress: the maximum force of deception and entropy that the corrected system must face. The three sinkings, the smoke, the Beast, and the sun from the West represent the systematic dismantling of the testing environment itself — the physical earth rupturing, the atmosphere filling, the final demarcation being drawn, the door of spiritual accountability closing.

The gentle wind represents divine mercy removing the faithful before the world's final degradation. The fire represents the final gathering of what remains. The trumpet represents the transition from test to verdict. Together, they form a sequence of absolute logical coherence: not dramatic chaos, but structured completion — a cosmos being brought to its designed conclusion with the precision of a Master who knew every step before the first one was taken.

THE COMPLETE SYSTEM — WHAT EACH SIGN ACCOMPLISHES

SIGNS 1-4 (Al-Mahdi, Dajjal, Isa, Gog & Magog): The testing of moral and epistemological loyalty — justice demonstrated, deception maximized, truth confirmed, entropy released and divinely terminated.

SIGNS 5-6 (Three Sinkings, Smoke): The physical dismantling of the testing environment — the arena itself begins collapsing. The earth ruptures; the atmosphere signals the end.

SIGN 7 (The Beast): Final demarcation — the permanent external marking of spiritual states. The examination results are posted. Ambiguity ends.

SIGN 8 (Sun from West): The door of accountability closes. No new faith. No new repentance. The ledger is sealed. The test is formally over.

SIGN 9 (Gentle Wind): Divine mercy removes the faithful before the world's ugliest hour. Allah does not make His servants witness what they do not need to witness.

SIGN 10 (Fire + Trumpet): Final gathering and the transition from the world of testing to the world of verdict. The symphony ends. The silence before the accounting begins.

The systemic reading reveals a design principle that runs through the entire End Times sequence: nothing is wasted, nothing is random, and every element performs a specific function in the moral and epistemological completion of the human story. The minor signs accumulate. The major signs execute. The remaining signs close. The trumpet sounds. The accounting begins. What looked from inside the experience like chaos was, from the perspective of the design, always a structured journey toward a conclusion that the Designer determined before the first human being was placed on the earth.

> كُلُّ نَفْسٍ ذَائِقَةُ الْمَوْتِ ۗ وَإِنَّمَا تُوَفَّوْنَ أُجُورَكُمْ يَوْمَ الْقِيَامَةِ
>
> *Kullu nafsin dha'iqatu al-mawt, wa innama tuwaffawna ujurakum yawma al-qiyamah*
>
> *"Every soul will taste death. And you will only be given your full compensation on the Day of Resurrection."*
>
> **Surah Aal-Imran, 3:185**

This verse — among the most frequently recited in the Islamic tradition — frames the entire human experience, including its eschatological conclusion, within the principle of deferred but certain compensation. Every soul will taste death. Every soul will receive its full accounting. The End Times sequence is the architecture of that receiving: the signs that mark the approach of the accounting, the closure of the testing environment, and the initiation of the verdict. Nothing is lost. Nothing is unaccounted. The promise is precise.

> *For the reader who has carried the weight of injustice — who has watched wrongs go unrighted, truth go unrecognized, and patience go unrewarded — the complete sequence of major signs is the most comprehensive answer the prophetic tradition offers: every account will be settled. Not in this world alone, and not through human mechanisms alone. In the most complete, most precise, most just accounting that any framework — religious or secular — has ever promised.*

LIVING IN THE CODA — WHAT THIS COMPLETE PICTURE DEMANDS

RECOGNITION: The minor signs accumulating around you are not background noise. They are the approach of the coda. Reading them accurately is itself an act of worship.

PREPARATION: The gentle wind takes a mustard seed of faith. The preparation required is not monumental achievement — it is the preservation of genuine moral orientation in an environment designed to erode it.

ACTION: Al-Mahdi's bay'ah does not emerge from passive populations. It emerges from communities that have maintained the capacity for justice-seeking even during the period of maximum entropy. Your choices now shape those communities.

TRUST: The sequence is complete. The design is coherent. The promise is certain. The specific timing belongs to divine knowledge alone — and that is not a frustration. It is a mercy. The uncertainty of timing is what makes the quality of living in the remaining measures matter.

The Coda Is Not the End — It Is the Completion

The remaining major signs are not postscripts to the main story. They are the main story's most honest chapter: the one that does not flinch from what the conclusion of a finite world, designed for testing, actually looks like. The physical earth ruptures. The sky fills with smoke. A Beast emerges to mark the final moral demarcation. The sun rises from the wrong direction and the door of repentance closes. A gentle wind takes every soul in which genuine good remains. A fire drives the rest to their gathering. A trumpet sounds.

And then: every soul standing. Looking. Waiting for the accounting that the entire sequence of history — from Adam's first breath to the last person herded by fire toward al-Mahshar — was always moving toward. The test is over. The examiner is present. The ledger is open. What each soul chose in the measures before the coda is what each soul carries into the accounting.

This is not a framework for despair. It is a framework for clarity. The sequence is complete. The logic is coherent. The promise is certain. The question that this book has been asking from its first chapter — whether a civilization that reads prophecy as a system rather than a story can extract from it the moral seriousness and practical wisdom it was designed to produce — finds its final answer here: yes. But only if the reading produces not anxiety about the signs but orientation toward what the signs are pointing to.

> *For every reader who has stayed with this book through its seven previous chapters — who has read the minor signs and felt the weight of recognition, who has studied Al-Mahdi's portrait and felt the stirring of hope, who has engaged the Dajjal's architecture and felt the sharpening of discernment, who has read of Isa's return and felt the deepest possible form of consolation — this chapter is not a conclusion. It is a beginning. The beginning of living, in whatever time remains, as though the coda matters. Because it does.*

The symphony was always going to end.

The question was never whether you would hear the final note.

It was what you did with every measure before it.

✦ ✦ ✦

Chapter Nine: Living in the Signs — A Framework for the Present Moment

continues on the following page...

CHAPTER NINE

Living in the Signs —

A Framework for the Present Moment

There is a particular kind of knowledge that changes the person who receives it. Not because it tells them something they could not have guessed, but because it reframes the context in which every subsequent choice is made. A doctor who receives a diagnosis does not simply receive information — they receive a new relationship with time. A soldier who is told the nature of the terrain ahead does not simply receive intelligence — they receive the conditions within which every subsequent decision must be navigated. What you know about where you are changes what it means to act.

This book has spent eight chapters building the most analytically rigorous, most authentically grounded, most systemically coherent reading of the End Times available to the present-day reader. The minor signs have been mapped as a diagnostic system. Al-Mahdi's portrait has been established with hadith precision and human depth. The Dajjal's architecture of deception has been analyzed as both individual threat and pre-terminal systemic condition. Isa ibn Maryam's descent has been placed in its full theological and comparative context. Gog and Magog have been understood as the final entropy that confirms the limits of human corrective capacity. And the remaining major signs have been read as the structured dissolution of the testing environment itself.

This ninth chapter asks the only question that makes all of that knowledge worth acquiring: what does it change? Not theoretically — practically. Not for scholars in seminaries or analysts in think-tanks, but for the father who wakes at 3 a.m. worried about what world his children are inheriting, the student who cannot reconcile what she knows with what she sees, the community leader who feels the weight of an era that seems to demand more clarity than any institution is producing, and the private person who simply wants to know how to live well in a time that the prophetic tradition has specifically, precisely, and honestly described as difficult.

> *For the reader who has stayed with this book not as an intellectual exercise but as a genuine search — who wanted not just to understand the End Times but to understand how to be a human being of integrity within them — this chapter is the book's most personal offering. Not a prescription. A framework.*

I. The First Error — Fatalism Disguised as Faith

The most common response to a comprehensive engagement with End Times narrations is one that presents itself as faith but functions as its opposite: fatalism. The reasoning runs as follows — if the signs are accumulating, if the trajectory is set, if Al-Mahdi will come regardless and the Dajjal will appear regardless and the trumpet will sound regardless, then what exactly is the point of human effort? The conclusion feels pious because it invokes divine sovereignty, but it is in fact a sophisticated form of moral abdication.

The prophetic tradition explicitly and emphatically refuses this conclusion. The same Prophet who described the signs of the Hour in such detail also said: 'If the Hour is established while one of you has a seedling in his hand, and he is able to plant it before the Hour overtakes him, let him plant it.' The juxtaposition is precise and deliberate: the Hour is imminent — plant the tree. Not despite the imminence. Because of it.

> *If the Hour is established while one of you has a seedling in his hand, and he is able to plant it before the Hour overtakes him, let him plant it.*
>
> — **Musnad Ahmad, Hadith 12902 — Sahih according to al-Albani and Shu'ayb al-Arnaut**

The analytical content of this hadith is extraordinary. It does not say 'plant the tree if you think you have time.' It says plant it even if the Hour is upon you — even if the last moment is now. Why? Because the value of the act is not contingent on whether the tree will grow to maturity, or whether any human being will eat its fruit, or whether civilization will continue long enough to benefit from it. The value of the act is in the act itself: the exercise of human moral agency, directed toward growth and benefit, in the very moment when entropy appears most absolute.

Fatalism mistakes the certainty of the sequence for the irrelevance of human choice within it. The sequence is certain — Al-Mahdi will come, the Dajjal will appear, the trumpet will sound. None of that is conditional on human effort. But who you are when those moments arrive is entirely conditional on what you chose in the measures before them. The sequence is fixed. Your position within it is not.

> *For the person who read the previous eight chapters and felt the approaching weight of inevitability — who felt the pull toward passivity, toward 'what can I do in a world heading this way' — the tree-planting hadith is the prophetic tradition's most direct and most counter-intuitive answer. Plant the tree. Especially now. Especially if the Hour is upon you.*

II. The Second Error — Obsession Disguised as Awareness

The opposite error from fatalism is equally destructive and equally common: eschatological obsession — the condition in which awareness of the signs becomes a replacement for living within them with integrity. The person afflicted by this condition spends their intellectual and emotional energy cataloguing signs, identifying the Dajjal in every powerful institution, and consuming eschatological content as a substitute for the moral and spiritual work that the tradition is actually demanding.

The Prophet Muhammad (peace be upon him) was asked repeatedly about the timing of the Hour. His response was consistent and instructive: he redirected the question from 'when' to 'what have you prepared.' The tradition's emphasis is never on the timing of the signs but on the quality of the person who will encounter them. The question that the entire eschatological framework is designed to generate is not 'is this the Dajjal?' but 'am I the kind of person who would recognize the Dajjal?'

> *A man asked: When is the Hour? The Prophet replied: What have you prepared for it? The man said: I have not prepared much prayer or fasting or charity, but I love Allah and His Messenger. The Prophet said: You will be with those you love.*
>
> **— Sahih al-Bukhari, Hadith 3688 — narrated by Anas ibn Malik (RA)**

This exchange is among the most humanly significant in the entire hadith literature. The man's answer is disarmingly honest: he has not prepared much in terms of formal religious performance.

What he has is love — genuine attachment to Allah and His Messenger. And the Prophet's response redirects the entire framework of eschatological preparation away from achievement and toward orientation. You will be with those you love. The criterion is not quantity of worship but direction of heart.

Eschatological obsession misreads this framework entirely. It focuses on the external content of the signs — who is the Dajjal, where is Al-Mahdi, which country is this hadith about — while neglecting the internal preparation that the tradition consistently identifies as the actual substance of readiness. A person who knows every hadith about the Dajjal but has not cultivated the depth perception to recognize deception in their own life has gained information without preparation.

FATALISM (Error of Passivity)	OBSESSION (Error of Hyperactivity)
'The trajectory is set — human effort is meaningless'	'Identifying signs' becomes a substitute for living them
Invokes divine sovereignty to justify moral abdication	Invokes prophetic knowledge to justify spiritual bypassing
Produces paralysis — nothing is worth doing	Produces anxiety — everything is a sign of something worse
The tree is not planted because 'what's the point'	The tree is discussed endlessly but never planted
Disconnected from human responsibility	Disconnected from human groundedness
Corrective: The seedling hadith — act regardless of imminence	Corrective: The 'what have you prepared' hadith — focus internally

The healthy response to End Times awareness navigates between these two errors: neither paralyzed by the weight of what is coming nor consumed by the preoccupation with identifying it. It holds the complete picture clearly — the signs, the sequence, the meaning — and then returns, every day, to the specific, local, proximate work of being a person of integrity in the particular life and community and moment that divine wisdom has placed them in.

III. What the Signs Are Actually Asking Of You

Each category of the minor and major signs, read with the analytical precision this book has attempted, generates a specific, practical demand on the person living in the period of their accumulation. These demands are not additional religious obligations layered onto the existing framework of Islamic practice. They are the application of that framework to the specific conditions the signs describe — the direction of existing capacities toward the vulnerabilities and challenges that the signs have identified.

SIGN / CATEGORY	WHAT IT DIAGNOSES	WHAT IT DEMANDS OF YOU
Rafa' al-'Ilm (withdrawal of genuine knowledge)	The collapse of deep scholarship; the rise of confident-sounding ignorance; the replacement of depth with viral reach	Invest in depth. Seek teachers, not influencers. Verify before sharing. Protect your epistemic environment with the same seriousness you protect your physical one.
Amanah collapse (trust betrayal institutionalized)	Every institution hollowing out while maintaining exterior form; authority given to the unworthy; the gap between public role and private reality widening	Be personally trustworthy to a degree that seems excessive for the environment. In an age of performed reliability, genuine amanah is radical. Your trustworthiness is the community's immune system.
Social fragmentation (kinship severed)	Atomization; loneliness epidemic; community replaced by online performance; the severing of the bonds that make moral accountability possible	Build and maintain real, proximate relationships. Physical presence. Regular contact. Communities that share meals and decisions and difficulties. The Dajjal cannot operate where genuine community exists.
Moral inversion (good called evil, evil called good)	The social cost of integrity rising; preference falsification	Develop the courage to hold positions based on evidence and conviction

	institutionalized; authentic moral expression becoming socially penalized	rather than social reward. Not aggression — clarity. The burning coal hadith describes the condition; the response is to hold it, not to put it down.
The Dajjal's pre-terminal system (one-eyed architecture)	Information ecosystems optimized for surface engagement; deepfake reality; manufactured consensus; the divorce of confidence from competence	Cultivate depth perception as a practice. Read Surah Al-Kahf weekly — not as superstition but as epistemic training. Distinguish between signal and noise. Value slowness and verification over speed and confidence.
The gentle wind (mustard seed threshold)	The minimum of genuine faith that qualifies for divine mercy at the world's end is not achievement but authenticity — genuine orientation toward the good, however imperfect	Protect the authenticity of your relationship with Allah above its performance. An imperfect, genuine faith is worth more than a polished, performed one. The wind takes what is real.

IV. The Discipline of Depth Perception

The single most practically consequential preparation for living in the period of the Dajjal's pre-terminal manifestations — and for recognizing the authentic from the counterfeit in the period of Al-Mahdi's emergence — is what this book has been calling depth perception: the cultivated capacity to see through surface presentation to underlying reality, to distinguish the authentic from its simulation, and to maintain epistemic orientation when the social and informational environment is systematically designed to undermine it.

Depth perception is not a natural gift. It is a cultivated discipline. The prophetic tradition prescribed its cultivation with remarkable specificity: the weekly recitation of Surah Al-Kahf, the daily seeking of refuge from the Dajjal's fitnah in the tashahhud of every prayer, the maintenance of connection with scholarly tradition, and the cultivation of genuine community as an epistemological support structure. Each of these prescriptions addresses one of the four attack vectors that the Dajjal's deception system — and its pre-terminal analogues — deploys against human epistemic integrity.

> *Whoever memorizes the first ten verses of Surah Al-Kahf will be protected from the Dajjal.*

— Sahih Muslim, Hadith 809 — narrated by Abu al-Darda' (RA)

The specification of Surah Al-Kahf's first ten verses as protection against the Dajjal has generated centuries of scholarly commentary on why these particular verses. The consensus understanding — articulated by Ibn Kathir, al-Nawawi, and al-Qurtubi among others — is that these opening verses establish the Quranic framework for resisting precisely the forms of deception that the Dajjal maximizes: the glorification of worldly adornment over divine reality (verse 7-8), the test of social pressure on genuine faith (the People of the Cave), and the framing of human life as a test rather than a possession. Memorizing them is the inscription of this framework into the reader's cognitive architecture — the most durable form of epistemic preparation.

> وَاصْبِرْ نَفْسَكَ مَعَ الَّذِينَ يَدْعُونَ رَبَّهُم بِالْغَدَاةِ وَالْعَشِيِّ
> يُرِيدُونَ وَجْهَهُ

Wasbir nafsaka ma'a alladhina yad'una Rabbahum bil-ghadati wal-'ashiyyi yuriduna wajhah

"And keep yourself patient with those who call upon their Lord in the morning and the evening, seeking His face."

Surah Al-Kahf, 18:28

This verse — from within the same Surah prescribed as protection against the Dajjal — encodes the communal dimension of depth perception. The patience prescribed is not individual endurance. It is the act of keeping yourself — literally, tethering yourself — to a community of people whose orientation is toward Allah. The depth perception that resists the Dajjal is not achievable in isolation. It is a communal capacity that emerges from environments of shared genuine worship, honest discourse, and mutual accountability. The verse is telling you to choose your social environment with the same intentionality that you would choose the quality of your air or water.

THE FOUR DISCIPLINES OF DEPTH PERCEPTION

DISCIPLINE 1 — SURAH AL-KAHF (Weekly):

Not as ritual but as epistemic training. The four stories address: social pressure on faith, material seduction, the limits of knowledge, and the right use of power. Each week's recitation reinscribes the framework that the Dajjal's system is designed to erode.

DISCIPLINE 2 — TASHAHHUD REFUGE (Daily, Every Prayer):

The Prophet prescribed seeking refuge from four things in the final sitting of every prayer: the punishment of the grave, the punishment of Hell, the fitnah of life and death, and the fitnah of the Dajjal. The daily inscription of this refuge is the spiritual equivalent of a daily systems check — confirming your orientation before the day's epistemic environment has its full effect.

DISCIPLINE 3 — GENUINE SCHOLARLY CONNECTION:

In the era of rafa' al-'ilm, finding and maintaining connection with genuine scholarship — not content creators who quote scholars, but actual engagement with the scholarly tradition — is an act of counter-cultural resistance. The tradition does not live in algorithms. It lives in chains of transmission from person to person.

DISCIPLINE 4 — COMMUNITY AS EPISTEMOLOGICAL INFRASTRUCTURE:

Regular, physical, honest community with people who are also trying to maintain depth perception. This is the Quranic prescription of Surah Al-Kahf 18:28 — tethering yourself to those whose orientation is toward Allah. Not a social club. A mutual support structure for maintaining reality contact in an environment designed to undermine it.

V. The Discipline of Justice — Preparing the Conditions for Al-Mahdi

One of the most analytically productive insights that the systemic reading of Al-Mahdi's emergence generates is the recognition that his arrival is not independent of the communities that preceded him. He does not descend from the heavens as Isa ibn Maryam will. He emerges from within the Muslim community — born, raised, and formed within the conditions that his community has produced. This means that the quality of the community in the period before his emergence is directly related to the conditions within which he will be formed and from which he will be recognized.

Al-Mahdi's bay'ah is given to him by the people of Makkah — or a group among them — who recognize him and insist upon his leadership. That recognition is not automatic. It requires a community capable of recognizing genuine justice and genuine leadership — a community that has not completely lost the capacity for authentic discernment. A community that has been entirely consumed by the moral inversion described in the minor signs, in which good is called evil and evil good, is a community that could not recognize Al-Mahdi even if he stood before it.

> *The best of generations is my generation, then those who follow them, then those who follow them.*
>
> **— Sahih al-Bukhari, Hadith 2652 — narrated by Ibn Masood (RA)**

The declining quality of generations described in this hadith is not an invitation to despair. It is a baseline from which the trajectory of renewal can be measured. Every generation that successfully resists the decline — that maintains genuine scholarship, authentic amanah, real community, and honest worship in the face of pressures designed to erode all of these — is a generation that is pushing back against the trajectory. It is not reversing the macro-level accumulation of signs. But it is building the communities within which the people who will recognize Al-Mahdi will be formed.

The practical implication is direct: your work toward justice in your specific community — the organization you run with genuine amanah, the scholarship you pursue with genuine depth, the relationships you maintain with genuine honesty — is not merely personal piety. It is civilizational preparation. The community that can produce the people who will recognize and support Al-Mahdi is built one genuine act of justice at a time, across generations, by people who will never know that their specific contribution mattered.

> إِنَّ اللَّهَ لَا يُضِيعُ أَجْرَ الْمُحْسِنِينَ
>
> *Inna Allaha la yudi'u ajra al-muhsinin*
>
> *"Indeed, Allah does not allow the reward of the doers of good to be lost."*
>
> **Surah At-Tawbah, 9:120**

This verse is the prophetic tradition's most direct answer to the person who asks whether their small, local, unrecognized acts of justice matter in the context of the enormous civilizational forces the End Times describe. They matter — not because they will individually turn the tide of the macro-level trajectory, but because Allah's accounting is precise to the individual act, and the reward for genuine goodness is not contingent on its visible effect. The mustard seed of genuine good that the gentle wind comes to collect was planted by someone who did not know it would be collected. It was planted because it was the right thing to plant.

> *For the community leader who has spent years building something genuine in a world that increasingly rewards the spectacular and the viral — who sometimes wonders whether the quiet, real work is worth it when the loud, performed version seems to succeed — this verse is the most honest reassurance the tradition offers. It does not promise visible success. It promises that nothing genuine is wasted.*

VI. The Discipline of Honest Engagement with the Present

The systemic framework of this book has consistently argued that the prophetic tradition's value is diagnostic: it identifies the conditions of a civilization in decline with a precision that secular frameworks cannot replicate, and it provides both a conceptual vocabulary for understanding those conditions and a practical orientation for living within them with integrity. But this diagnostic value is only accessible to those who are willing to engage honestly with both the tradition and the present moment.

Honest engagement with the present means neither catastrophizing nor normalizing. Catastrophizing — treating every news event as a fulfilled prophecy, every crisis as the definitive threshold — has been the eschatological community's most consistent failure mode and has produced generations of false certainty followed by disillusionment. Normalizing — treating the accumulation of signs as background noise that does not require any adjustment to how one lives — has been modernity's most consistent failure mode, producing the comfortable numbness that the minor signs' accumulation is designed to puncture.

The middle path is what might be called calibrated alertness: a sustained awareness of where we are in the sequence, without the anxiety that comes from false certainty about timing, and without the complacency that comes from pretending the sequence is not advancing. This is the state the Prophet Muhammad (peace be upon him) was modeling when he described the signs in such detail: not to produce panic, but to produce the kind of informed, grounded moral seriousness that makes genuine preparation possible.

> *Be in this world as though you are a stranger or a traveler passing through.*

— Sahih al-Bukhari, Hadith 6416 — narrated by Abdullah ibn Umar (RA)

The traveler analogy is among the most practically precise in the entire hadith literature for living in the period of sign accumulation. A traveler does not invest in permanent structures at a way-station. They do not accumulate possessions that cannot be carried. They maintain awareness of their destination, they make use of what the way-station offers, and they do not confuse the stop with the journey's end. But — and this is the analogy's crucial dimension — a good traveler is fully present at each stop. They notice what is around them. They help fellow travelers. They rest when they need to and move when they must. They are not distracted by the destination to the point of missing the present moment.

Living in the signs means inhabiting the present fully — your specific family, your specific community, your specific work, your specific moment of history — with the awareness that this particular stop is not the destination and that the quality of how you travel matters more than the comfort of the stop.

> *For the young person who feels the weight of this moment in history — who senses that the world they are inheriting is structurally different from the one their parents inherited, and who wonders whether the frameworks that served previous generations are sufficient — the traveler hadith is not a counsel of detachment. It is a counsel of presence: be fully here, invest genuinely in what is real, and hold the whole picture with the clarity of someone who knows the journey's destination without pretending to know the exact route.*

VII. The Role of Knowledge in the Period of Its Withdrawal

The minor sign of rafa' al-'ilm — the withdrawal of genuine knowledge — places a specific and heightened obligation on those who, in the period of its decline, still have access to authentic scholarship. In a period when knowledge is being withdrawn through the death of scholars and the rise of confident ignorance, the preservation, transmission, and honest communication of genuine knowledge becomes an act of civilizational resistance.

This does not mean that every Muslim must become a hadith scholar or a jurist. It means that every Muslim who has access to genuine knowledge — whether of the Islamic sciences, of secular disciplines engaged honestly and deeply, or of the practical wisdom that genuine experience produces — carries a heightened responsibility to transmit it faithfully rather than to simplify it for palatability, embellish it for engagement, or abandon it for the social rewards of confident-sounding ignorance.

> *Convey from me, even if it is one verse.*

— **Sahih al-Bukhari, Hadith 3461 — narrated by Abdullah ibn Amr (RA)**

The minimal threshold — even one verse — is the prophetic tradition's democratic epistemology in its most concentrated form. You do not need to be a scholar to participate in the transmission of knowledge. You need to transmit what you actually know, with honesty about its scope and its limits, to the people around you who need it. In a period of rafa' al-'ilm, the person who transmits one genuine piece of verified truth to one person who needed it has participated in the counter-movement to the sign's trajectory.

The discipline of honest intellectual transmission also requires the courage to say 'I don't know.' In a period when confidence is rewarded and uncertainty is penalized — when the social incentive is to always have an answer — the person who says 'scholars differ on this and I am not qualified to resolve the difference' is performing an act of intellectual integrity that is counter-cultural, epistemologically essential, and directly prophylactic against the conditions the Dajjal will exploit.

> وَلَا تَقْفُ مَا لَيْسَ لَكَ بِهِ عِلْمٌ ۚ إِنَّ السَّمْعَ وَالْبَصَرَ
> وَالْفُؤَادَ كُلُّ أُولَٰئِكَ كَانَ عَنْهُ مَسْئُولًا

Wa la taqfu ma laysa laka bihi 'ilm, inna al-sam'a wal-basara wal-fu'ada kullu ula'ika kana 'anhu mas'ula

"And do not pursue that of which you have no knowledge. Indeed, the hearing, the sight, and the heart — about all those one will be questioned."

Surah Al-Isra, 17:36

This verse — the Quran's most direct epistemological commandment — is the foundation of the intellectual discipline that the period of rafa' al-'ilm demands. Do not pursue what you do not know: do not speak with authority you do not have, do not transmit what you have not verified, do not allow the social pressure to have an answer to override the honest acknowledgment that you do not. The hearing, the sight, and the heart will all be questioned — meaning that what you took in, what you chose to look at, and what you genuinely believed are all part of the account. Epistemic integrity is not an optional intellectual virtue. It is a component of moral accountability.

VIII. Raising Children in the Time of Signs

Perhaps the most acute application of the framework this book has been building is the question that many parents carry silently: how do you raise children of genuine faith, genuine depth, and genuine moral integrity in an environment whose systems are actively designed to produce the opposite? This is not an abstract concern. For many parents reading this book, it is the most pressing practical question they face.

The prophetic tradition's answer to this question is both counter-intuitive and deeply practical. It does not begin with protecting children from the environment — though appropriate protection has its place. It begins with building within the child the depth perception, the epistemic grounding, and the genuine relational experience of faith that makes the environment's influence navigable rather than determinative.

> *Every child is born in a state of fitra (natural disposition toward truth). It is his parents who make him a Jew, a Christian, or a Zoroastrian.*

— Sahih al-Bukhari, Hadith 1385 — narrated by Abu Hurairah (RA)

The fitra hadith is among the most cited in Islamic theology, but its practical implication for child-rearing in the period of sign accumulation deserves specific attention. The fitra — the natural disposition toward truth, toward the divine, toward genuine moral orientation — is present in every child at birth. The environment does not create it. The environment either cultivates it or suppresses it. The parent's role is not to install the fitra but to protect the conditions in which it can develop into genuine, durable faith.

In a period when the environment is maximally hostile to fitra — when the information ecosystem rewards surface engagement over depth, when social structures fragment community rather than build it, and when the models of authority that children encounter are consistently performing rather than genuinely leading — the cultivation of fitra requires deliberate, counter-cultural investment in the specific conditions that allow it to develop: genuine worship experienced rather than observed, genuine community lived rather than theorized, genuine knowledge transmitted with honesty about its limits, and genuine moral integrity modeled in the private moments as consistently as in the public ones.

> *For the parent who looks at their child and wonders whether what they are giving them is enough — whether the faith they have managed to transmit will hold in a world that seems designed to dissolve it — the fitra hadith is not reassurance that everything will be fine. It is the honest identification of where the work actually lies: not in the child's external protection but in the cultivation of the internal capacity that no environment can fully override if it has been genuinely developed.*

RAISING CHILDREN OF DEPTH IN A ONE-EYED ERA

WORSHIP AS EXPERIENCE, NOT OBSERVATION:

Children who pray alongside parents from childhood do not learn religion as a set of rules. They learn it as a lived orientation. The experience of genuine worship — felt, not merely performed — is the deepest inoculation against the Dajjal's surface-only reality.

GENUINE COMMUNITY AS NORMATIVE ENVIRONMENT:

Children need to experience community in which trust is real, honesty is expected, and adults practice what they teach. If the only genuine community in a child's life is online, the Dajjal's one-eyed architecture will feel like reality and everything else will feel like the aberration.

MODELING EPISTEMIC INTEGRITY:

A parent who says 'I don't know' when they don't know, who verifies before asserting, who engages with difficulty honestly rather than deflecting it — this parent is teaching depth perception as a lived practice. Children learn how to know things from watching how the adults around them treat the act of knowing.

THE QURAN AS RELATIONSHIP, NOT RECITATION:

The child who has heard the Quran discussed as a living address to their actual situation — whose questions about its meaning have been taken seriously, whose doubts have been engaged rather than silenced — has a relationship with the text that will survive the environments designed to sever it.

HONEST ENGAGEMENT WITH DIFFICULTY:

The parent who engages honestly with the hard questions — why does evil exist, why do the unjust prosper, why does the world seem to reward what is wrong — is building in their child the intellectual resilience that cheap answers produce the opposite of.

IX. The Community That Produces Al-Mahdi's Recognition

The systemic insight at the heart of this chapter — and at the heart of the entire book — is that Al-Mahdi's emergence is not independent of the community that precedes it. He emerges from within the Muslim community. He is recognized by people whose capacity for recognition has been cultivated. He is given bay'ah by a group whose capacity for genuine covenant has survived the conditions designed to destroy it. The community that produces that recognition is built not by eschatological speculation but by the daily, unglamorous, structurally necessary work of maintaining genuine depth in a world of surfaces.

This means that every teacher who teaches with genuine depth rather than algorithmic popularity is preparing conditions. Every scholar who maintains intellectual honesty at professional cost is preparing conditions. Every community leader who organizes around genuine mutual care rather than institutional performance is preparing conditions. Every parent who cultivates their child's fitra rather than their social compliance is preparing conditions. None of them will know, in their lifetime, whether their specific contribution helped produce the community in which Al-Mahdi will be recognized. That uncertainty is itself the test.

> *Actions are by their intentions, and every person will have what they intended.*
> **— Sahih al-Bukhari, Hadith 1 — narrated by Umar ibn al-Khattab (RA)**

The hadith of intentions — the first hadith in Sahih al-Bukhari, and traditionally the first hadith taught to every student of the Islamic sciences — is placed here deliberately. In a framework where the visible outcomes of human effort are uncertain and often invisible, the principle that actions are assessed by their intentions returns the locus of accountability to where it has always belonged: not to results, but to orientation. The person who builds genuine community with a genuine intention toward justice is credited for that intention, whether or not they live to see the community they built recognize Al-Mahdi.

The road map of Al-Mahdi in the End Times is not merely a description of what will happen. It is a description of the kind of human agency that the divine design has always been calling forth — the agency of people who build what is true in the time before it is needed, who maintain what is real when the environment is designed to make unreality feel normal, and who plant trees in the full knowledge that the Hour may arrive before the fruit is ready.

> *For every person who has felt the weight of living in a time that seems designed to make genuine faith, genuine depth, and genuine justice structurally difficult — and who has continued anyway — this framework is not a reward for your effort. It is the recognition that your effort is precisely what the design of this moment requires. The minor signs describe a world that needs exactly what you have been building. Keep building it.*

The Framework, Distilled

Nine chapters of analysis, authentication, and systemic reasoning have been building toward this: a framework for living in the present moment that takes the prophetic tradition with full seriousness — not as a source of anxiety about what is coming, but as a source of clarity about what is being asked.

The signs are not asking you to calculate the timing of Al-Mahdi's arrival. They are asking you to be the kind of person who would recognize him. The Dajjal is not asking you to identify which institution is his proxy. He is asking whether your depth perception is cultivated enough to function when the surface presentation is maximally compelling. The gentle wind's mustard seed is not asking you to achieve great religiosity. It is asking whether what you have is genuine.

The roadmap of Al-Mahdi in the End Times, read with analytical precision and human honesty, is not a map of events to observe. It is a map of conditions to inhabit — conditions that call for specific human responses, specific disciplines, specific communal structures, and a specific quality of moral seriousness that the accumulation of signs makes not merely desirable but urgent. The urgency is not panic. It is the urgency of the person who knows both where the journey ends and that what happens between here and there is not predetermined by the destination.

LIVING IN THE SIGNS — THE FRAMEWORK DISTILLED

KNOW THE SEQUENCE: Not to obsess over it, but to inhabit the present with the clarity of someone who understands the context. The signs are a diagnostic, not a script.

AVOID THE TWO ERRORS: Neither fatalism ('what's the point') nor obsession ('everything is a sign'). Both disconnect you from the specific, local work that your specific moment requires.

CULTIVATE DEPTH PERCEPTION: Surah Al-Kahf weekly. Tashahhud refuge daily. Genuine scholarly connection. Real community. These are not additional obligations — they are the specific preparation the tradition prescribes for the specific vulnerabilities the signs identify.

BUILD JUSTICE LOCALLY: Al-Mahdi's community is built one genuine act of integrity at a time. Your trustworthiness, your honest knowledge transmission, your genuine community-building — these are civilizational preparation, not private piety.

RAISE DEPTH, NOT COMPLIANCE: The fitra is present in every child. Your role is to cultivate the conditions in which it develops into genuine, durable faith — not to impose external compliance that dissolves under the first real pressure.

PLANT THE TREE: Even if the Hour is upon you. Especially then. The value of the act is not contingent on whether the fruit will be eaten. It is in the orientation of the planting.

The signs are not asking you to predict what is coming.
They are asking you to become the kind of person
who was worth the preparation that the signs describe.

✦ ✦ ✦

Chapter Ten: The Roadmap Completed — Justice, Truth, and the Human Story

continues on the following page...

CHAPTER TEN
The Roadmap Completed —
Justice, Truth, and the Human Story

There is a moment, near the end of any great journey, when the traveler turns and sees the entire road behind them for the first time as a whole. Individual stages that seemed disconnected — the steep ascent, the valley of confusion, the long plateau, the sudden descent — resolve into a single coherent path. The difficulty of each stage was not arbitrary. It was the precise preparation for what came next. The road was designed.

We have traveled ten chapters. We began with the foundational claim that prophetic eschatology is not a dramatic narrative but a diagnostic system — a structured framework for understanding civilizational collapse and divine correction. We mapped the minor signs as the measurable degradation of a civilization's moral and epistemic infrastructure. We established Al-Mahdi's authenticated portrait with hadith precision and studied his bay'ah as the system's bifurcation point. We analyzed the Dajjal as both individual threat and pre-terminal systemic condition, and Isa ibn Maryam as the truth whose presence the deception system cannot survive. We engaged Gog and Magog as the final proof that the correction's limit lies beyond human agency, and the remaining major signs as the structured dissolution of the testing environment. And we asked, in Chapter Nine, the only question that makes all of that knowledge worth having: what does it change?

This final chapter does not introduce new material. It does what the final chapter of a serious work must do: it holds the entire roadmap in view simultaneously and asks what the complete picture means — for the understanding of justice, for the understanding of truth, for the understanding of the human story itself. And it offers, as its final gift to the reader, the recognition that this roadmap was not written for scholars alone. It was written for every human being who has ever looked at the world and asked whether its trajectory makes sense.

> *For the reader who began this book with intellectual curiosity and arrives at this final chapter carrying something heavier and more personal — a recognition of where we are, a seriousness about what is being asked, a renewed relationship with the tradition that produced this roadmap — the journey has worked. That weight is not a burden. It is the beginning of clarity.*

I. What the Roadmap Reveals About Justice

The most consistent theme across the entire End Times sequence — the thread that runs from Al-Mahdi's bay'ah through Isa ibn Maryam's governance to the gentle wind's mercy — is justice. Not justice as an abstract political value, but justice as a systemic operating principle: the specific quality of social organization in which every element of the system — material, epistemic, relational, spiritual — functions according to its designed purpose rather than its corrupted deviation from it.

The Islamic concept of adl — justice — is not primarily about legal equality, though it includes it. It is about putting everything in its proper place: giving to each thing the station, the weight, and the treatment that its actual nature deserves. Zulm — oppression, injustice — is, etymologically, the placing of something in a position it does not belong: the unworthy in authority, the false in the position of truth, the powerful where the righteous should stand, the counterfeit where the genuine should be honored. The entire minor signs catalogue is a description of a civilization practicing zulm at scale — misplacing everything that matters.

> إِنَّ اللَّهَ يَأْمُرُ بِالْعَدْلِ وَالْإِحْسَانِ وَإِيتَاءِ ذِي الْقُرْبَىٰ
> وَيَنْهَىٰ عَنِ الْفَحْشَاءِ وَالْمُنكَرِ وَالْبَغْيِ ۚ يَعِظُكُمْ لَعَلَّكُمْ
> تَذَكَّرُونَ

Inna Allaha ya'muru bil-'adli wal-ihsani wa-ita'i dhil-qurba wa yanha 'ani al-fahsha'i wal-munkari wal-baghi, ya'izukum la'allakum tadhakkarun

"Indeed, Allah commands justice, good conduct, and giving to relatives; and forbids immorality, bad conduct, and oppression. He admonishes you that perhaps you will be reminded."

Surah An-Nahl, 16:90

This verse — cited in Chapter One as the Quranic definition of a healthy civilization's operating conditions — returns here at the book's conclusion with its full weight. The End Times sequence is, in its totality, the story of what happens when these three commands (adl, ihsan, giving to kin) are progressively abandoned and the three prohibitions (immorality, bad conduct, oppression) progressively institutionalized — and then the story of their restoration. Al-Mahdi's mission is Surah An-Nahl 16:90 reimplemented as a civilizational operating system after generations of its systematic dismantling.

What the roadmap reveals about justice is this: justice is not fragile. It appears fragile because its enemies are persistent and its defenders are often exhausted. But the entire trajectory of the End Times sequence — from the minor signs' accumulation through the major signs' resolution — demonstrates that justice is not something that can be permanently extinguished. It can be deferred, suppressed, counterfeited, and driven underground. But it cannot be eliminated. The divine design guarantees its eventual restoration — through Al-Mahdi's bay'ah, through Isa's governance, through the worm in Gog and Magog's neck, through the trumpet's second blast and the accounting that follows. Justice is the destination of the entire human journey. The question is only the route.

> *For every person who has fought for justice in their specific corner of the world and felt the weight of how slowly it moves — how stubborn injustice is, how quickly gains are reversed, how exhausting the maintenance of integrity is in environments designed to erode it — the complete roadmap is the most honest reassurance available: you are not wrong about justice's importance. You are simply living in the middle of the story, not at its end.*

II. What the Roadmap Reveals About Truth

The second great theme of the End Times sequence is truth — not truth as a philosophical category but truth as a force with structural properties. The Dajjal's entire architecture is built on the premise that truth can be permanently replaced by its simulation — that a sufficiently sophisticated counterfeit, delivered with sufficient confidence and material reinforcement, can function as a complete substitute for reality. The defeat of the Dajjal is the empirical refutation of this premise at civilizational scale.

What the Dajjal's dissolution at the mere sight of Isa ibn Maryam reveals is a principle the Quran has encoded repeatedly: falsehood carries within it the mechanism of its own dissolution. It does not merely lose contests with truth — it loses the capacity to exist in truth's undistorted presence. The simulation cannot survive the return of what it was simulating. Al-Masih al-Dajjal — the false Messiah — dissolves before Al-Masih Isa ibn Maryam — the true one. The correspondence is exact and deliberate.

> وَقُلْ جَاءَ الْحَقُّ وَزَهَقَ الْبَاطِلُ ۚ إِنَّ الْبَاطِلَ كَانَ زَهُوقًا
>
> *Wa qul ja'a al-haqqu wa zahaqa al-batilu, inna al-batila kana zahuqa*
>
> *"And say: Truth has come, and falsehood has departed. Indeed, falsehood is ever bound to depart."*
>
> **Surah Al-Isra, 17:81**

This verse — cited in the book's opening chapter as a systems law — returns here with its meaning fully demonstrated by everything the intervening chapters have shown. The Dajjal is the terminal expression of al-batil: falsehood at its most organized, most resourced, and most persuasive. And he is zahiq — departed, dissolved — in the presence of al-haqq embodied in Isa ibn Maryam. The verse is not poetic reassurance. It is a structural law of reality that the entire End Times sequence exists to demonstrate at maximum scale.

What the roadmap reveals about truth is this: truth does not win by being more persuasive than falsehood. In any contest of persuasiveness, falsehood — with its superior flexibility, its freedom from the constraint of accuracy, and its capacity to tell people what they want to hear — will often win in the short term. Truth wins by being what it is: the underlying structure of reality that every simulation must eventually fail to replicate. The Dajjal's deception works until Isa arrives. Then it simply stops working. Not because it was defeated in argument. Because it encountered a presence it could not simulate.

> *For the person who has felt, in their own life, the exhaustion of arguing for truth against a confident, well-*

> *resourced falsehood — who has wondered whether the truth has any advantage in an era when persuasiveness is decoupled from accuracy — the Dajjal's dissolution is the prophetic tradition's most direct answer. In the long run, the only run that ultimately matters, truth does not need to win the argument. It only needs to show up.*

III. What the Roadmap Reveals About the Human Story

The secular frameworks that have dominated intellectual life since the Enlightenment tell a story about human history that is, at its core, a story of progress — linear, developmental, and ultimately optimistic about human capacity. The religious frameworks that preceded them told a story of fall and redemption — cyclical, dependent on divine intervention, and ultimately optimistic about divine mercy rather than human capacity. The prophetic eschatological framework of the End Times belongs to neither category entirely, and its refusal to fit either template is one of the most analytically significant things about it.

The End Times roadmap is not a story of progress. The minor signs describe unambiguous civilizational decline — the erosion of the qualities that make human community function justly. But it is not a simple story of fall and divine rescue either. Al-Mahdi is a human being. His bay'ah is a human covenant. His governance is a human exercise of justice. The correction is divinely facilitated but humanly executed. The story the roadmap tells is something more complex: a story of human agency operating within divine design, capable of genuine achievement precisely because it is operating within a framework that guarantees the ultimate victory of what it is trying to achieve.

> وَلَقَدْ كَتَبْنَا فِي الزَّبُورِ مِن بَعْدِ الذِّكْرِ أَنَّ الْأَرْضَ
> يَرِثُهَا عِبَادِيَ الصَّالِحُونَ

Wa laqad katabna fi al-Zaburi min ba'di al-dhikri anna al-arda yarithuha 'ibadiya al-salihun

"And We have already written in the Psalms, after the mention of the Torah, that the earth is inherited by My righteous servants."

Surah Al-Anbiya, 21:105

This verse — the divine inscription across revelatory traditions that the righteous will ultimately inherit the earth — is the Quranic statement of the human story's ultimate trajectory. It is not a promise of inevitable progress through human effort alone. It is a promise that the divine design has already written the final chapter, and that chapter belongs to those who, in the middle chapters, chose righteousness. The entire End Times roadmap is the mechanism through which this written promise is delivered.

What the roadmap reveals about the human story is this: it is a story that was always going somewhere. The apparent chaos of history — the rise and fall of civilizations, the triumph of injustice and its eventual undoing, the accumulation of signs and the arrival of corrections — is not random. It is a structured journey toward a destination that was determined before the first step was taken. The human contribution to that journey is not the destination — it is the quality of the traveling. And the quality of the traveling, the prophetic tradition insists with extraordinary precision, matters eternally.

IV. The Universal Dimension — Speaking Across Traditions

One of the most analytically significant properties of the End Times roadmap, as established across the preceding chapters, is its cross-traditional resonance. The Abrahamic traditions — Islam, Christianity, and Judaism — converge around the same basic eschatological architecture: a period of maximum moral and social degradation, the emergence or return of a divinely-commissioned figure of justice and truth, the defeat of the supreme deceiver, and a final accounting. The specific theological frameworks differ, sometimes irreconcilably. The structural expectation is remarkably convergent.

This convergence is not accidental, and it is not merely the result of one tradition borrowing from another. It reflects the Islamic theological position that the divine guidance transmitted through all the prophets was, at its core, one guidance — one message, one moral direction, one eschatological trajectory. The differences between the traditions are real and significant. But the deep structural convergence around the questions of justice, truth, and the final resolution of the human story is the signature of a single divine Author addressing the same human condition across multiple cultural and linguistic contexts.

THE UNIVERSAL ESCHATOLOGICAL CONVERGENCE

THE SHARED ARCHITECTURE ACROSS TRADITIONS:

All three Abrahamic traditions expect: a period of unprecedented moral crisis preceding the resolution; a divinely-commissioned figure who restores justice or judges the world; the defeat of a supreme force of deception; and a final accounting in which every act is weighed.

THE SHARED FIGURE: Isa ibn Maryam / Jesus Christ / The Messiah awaited by Judaism — three traditions, one figure at the center of the eschatological resolution. The theological frameworks around him differ fundamentally. The convergence of expectation is undeniable.

WHAT CONVERGENCE MEANS: Not that the traditions are the same — they are not, and their differences must not be dissolved. It means that the human condition the traditions address is the same, and the divine diagnosis of that condition's terminal expression and ultimate resolution shares a structural logic that transcends the specific theological vocabulary of any single tradition.

THE ISLAMIC POSITION: The convergence is expected, because the Quran affirms that every prophet brought the same essential guidance. The differences are the result of human alteration of divine revelation over time. The underlying roadmap was always one roadmap, delivered in stages, culminating in the final delivery through Muhammad (pbuh) and the final application through Isa ibn Maryam (pbuh).

For the secular reader — who has no stake in any of the three traditions but who finds the structural convergence analytically striking — the question the roadmap raises is a genuinely serious one: what does it mean that the three traditions that have shaped the moral imagination of the majority of human beings across most of recorded history converge, independently and across significant theological differences, around the same basic diagnosis of the human condition's terminal crisis and the same basic structure of its resolution? The question is not answered by dismissing it as coincidence. It is answered by engaging it with the analytical seriousness it deserves.

> *For the reader who belongs to none of these traditions but who feels, in the 21st century's particular combination of technological power and moral confusion, the reality of a world that seems simultaneously more capable and less wise than any before it — the roadmap is not asking for your theological commitment. It is offering you a framework for understanding what you are already experiencing. The diagnosis does not require the tradition. But the tradition offers the most complete diagnosis available.*

V. The Unique Contribution of the Systemic Reading

This book has argued, from its opening chapter, that the End Times tradition has been consistently underserved by the two dominant modes of its presentation: popular sensationalism, which reduces it to a catalogue of dramatic events for emotional consumption, and academic detachment, which analyzes it as a textual and historical artifact without engaging its meaning for the present moment. The systemic reading proposed and developed across these ten chapters represents a third mode — one that takes the authenticated tradition with full scholarly seriousness while reading it with the analytical tools that allow its diagnostic value to be fully realized.

The key moves of the systemic reading can now be stated in their complete form. First: the minor signs are not isolated prophecies but a connected map of systemic degradation — a civilization's self-destruction charted across five mutually reinforcing categories of failure. Second: Al-Mahdi, the Dajjal, and Isa ibn Maryam are not sequential characters but systemic forces — each representing a distinct phase in the correction cycle of a civilization that has reached terminal moral and epistemic failure. Third: the major signs are not dramatic interruptions of history but the structured dissolution of the testing environment — each sign performing a specific function in the orderly completion of the human examination. Fourth: the framework's value is not in predicting timing but in generating the moral seriousness and practical wisdom that the tradition was always designed to produce.

WHAT POPULAR TREATMENTS MISS	**WHAT THIS BOOK'S READING ADDS**
The systemic connections between signs. The authenticated portrait vs. the embellished mythology. The practical demands the tradition generates. The diagnostic value for the present moment.	The minor signs as a connected degradation map. Al-Mahdi as systemic corrective, not political messiah. The Dajjal as both individual and pre-terminal force. The complete sequence as structured, purposive design.
WHAT ACADEMIC TREATMENTS MISS	**WHAT THE TRADITION ITSELF DEMANDS**
The tradition's diagnostic value for the present. The human depth of the prophetic portrait. The practical framework for living within the signs. The universal convergence across traditions.	Authentic narrations only, with grading transparent. Scholarly differences honestly presented. No fabrication, no prediction, no sect bias. And above all: a reading that changes how you live.

VI. The Questions This Book Cannot Answer

Intellectual honesty requires, in a final chapter, the acknowledgment of what this book has not and cannot resolve. The limits of the analysis are as important as its content, and presenting them transparently is itself an act of the intellectual integrity that the tradition demands.

This book cannot tell you when Al-Mahdi will appear. The Prophet Muhammad (peace be upon him) did not specify this, and any attempt to calculate it from the signs — however sophisticated the methodology — produces false certainty about what the tradition has deliberately left uncertain. The timing belongs to divine knowledge alone, and the tradition's deliberate silence on it is not an oversight. It is a mercy: the uncertainty of timing is what makes the quality of every present moment matter.

This book cannot tell you where Al-Mahdi currently is, or whether he has been born, or what his specific identity will be until the bay'ah reveals him. The authenticated narrations describe him by name type, lineage, character, and mission — not by current location or biographical details that would allow pre-identification. Any claim to have identified Al-Mahdi before his bay'ah is, by the tradition's own criteria, false: the man who does not seek the role cannot be identified by observers before the community insists upon it.

This book cannot resolve the scholarly differences that remain genuinely open: the precise branch of Al-Mahdi's lineage (Hasani or Husayni), the exact sequence of events in the period immediately surrounding his emergence, the specific identity of Gog and Magog, and the precise location of Dhul-Qarnayn's barrier. These are questions on which classical scholars of the highest caliber have disagreed, and the disagreement reflects the genuine limits of the textual evidence. To pretend otherwise would be to do exactly what the tradition warns against: speaking with authority one does not possess.

> *Say: My Lord, increase me in knowledge.*

— Surah Ta-Ha, 20:114 — this Quranic supplication is itself the tradition's prescription for the state of acknowledged partial knowledge: not to pretend completeness, but to continue seeking.

What the book can offer — and what it has attempted to offer across ten chapters — is the most rigorous, most authentically grounded, most analytically productive reading of the End Times framework that a faithful engagement with both the prophetic tradition and the tools of serious intellectual analysis can produce. That is enough. It is, in fact, more than enough to change how a person lives. And changing how a person lives is what the tradition was always designed to do.

VII. The Book's Core Claim — Restated in Full

This book began with a claim that it has spent ten chapters substantiating: that the End Times tradition, read as a system rather than a story, possesses a diagnostic and prescriptive power that neither its popular treatments nor its academic analyses have fully realized. That claim can now be restated in its complete form.

The prophetic tradition's eschatological framework is a comprehensive diagnosis of what happens to human civilization when it progressively abandons the operating principles that divine guidance was designed to maintain — and a precise description of the correction sequence through which those operating principles are ultimately restored. The minor signs are the diagnostic data. Al-Mahdi is the first corrective intervention. The Dajjal is the maximum resistance of the corrupted system. Isa ibn Maryam is the completion of the correction. Gog and Magog are the proof that the corrected system's limits lie beyond human agency. The remaining major signs are the structured dissolution of the testing environment. And the trumpet is the transition from test to verdict.

Read this way, the tradition is not primarily about prediction. It is about pattern recognition — the capacity to identify where a civilization is in its corruption cycle, what the dynamics of its situation are, and what the specific demands of that situation are on the people living within it. The person who has genuinely absorbed the systemic reading of the End Times tradition is not primarily a person who knows when things will happen. They are a person who knows what kind of person to be in the time before they do.

THE ROADMAP — COMPLETE SYNTHESIS

The human story is a test, not a drift.

The test has a structure, not a random sequence of events.

The structure was designed to produce specific human responses: justice, truth, depth, community, and covenant.

Al-Mahdi is the human correction — the proof that justice, when it reaches critical moral mass, produces the leader capable of implementing it.

The Dajjal is the system's maximum resistance — the proof that deception, however sophisticated, cannot survive the presence of what it was simulating.

Isa ibn Maryam is the completion — the return of the original in the presence of which the counterfeit dissolves.

Gog and Magog are the limit — the proof that the correction's final resolution lies beyond human agency.

The remaining signs are the closure — the structured end of the testing environment and the preparation for the final accounting.

— And you are living in the middle of this.

— Not at the end. Not before the beginning. In the accumulation.

— The question is not when the signs will complete their sequence.

— The question is what you are doing with the time before they do.

VIII. Five Human Faces of the Present Moment

Abstract frameworks, however analytically rigorous, need the weight of human specificity to become more than intellectual structures. This book has attempted throughout to maintain the human dimension alongside the analytical one. In this final section, five specific human situations are named — not as case studies but as recognitions: the people this book was ultimately written for.

FIVE HUMAN FACES OF LIVING IN THE SIGNS

THE SCHOLAR WHO FEELS THE WEIGHT OF THE TRADITION:

You have spent years in the texts. You know the authentic from the fabricated. You have watched the tradition's depth being replaced by its performance. This book is written for you as a reminder that the depth you carry is not yours alone — it belongs to the chain of transmission that runs from the Prophet (pbuh) through every honest scholar to you, and through you to whoever you reach. Carry it faithfully.

THE PARENT WHO WONDERS IF IT IS ENOUGH:

You have done what you could: the prayers witnessed, the Quran read, the honest conversations about difficulty. You are not sure it took hold. The fitra hadith says: what you planted is there. The gentle wind collects a mustard seed. Trust the harvest to the One who designed the fitra.

THE YOUNG PERSON INHERITING A FRACTURED WORLD:

You were born into a world whose institutions arrived already hollowed out, whose information environment was already optimized for engagement over truth, whose community structures were already atomized. None of that is your fault. All of it is your inheritance — and your opportunity. The generation that was born into the accumulation is the generation that gets to choose, in full knowledge of the signs, what to build anyway.

THE SEEKER FROM ANOTHER TRADITION:

You arrived at this book not as a Muslim but as someone whose own tradition has brought you to the same questions: the crisis of meaning, the triumph of deception, the search for a framework that explains the world's trajectory without pretending it is not dark. The roadmap does not ask for your conversion. It asks for your honest engagement with the questions it raises. Those questions belong to every human being.

THE PERSON WHO SIMPLY WANTS TO LIVE WELL:

You are not a scholar. You are not an activist. You are a person who wakes up each morning, raises a family or builds something or serves people in some capacity, and wants to do it with integrity in a time that makes integrity structurally difficult. This book is most fundamentally for you. The mustard seed is real. The tree is worth planting. The traveler's presence at the way-station matters, even if the journey continues beyond it.

IX. The Tradition Speaks — Its Final Word to the Present

The Prophet Muhammad (peace be upon him) described the signs of the Hour across his entire prophetic mission — not in a single comprehensive discourse but in responses to questions, in warnings delivered to companions, in dreams and visions shared with those who would transmit them, and in the ordinary conversations of a prophetic life that was simultaneously the most human and the most divinely guided that history has recorded. The accumulation of those descriptions, preserved across fourteen centuries of scholarly transmission, constitutes the most comprehensive map of the present moment that any tradition has produced.

The map was not drawn for the generation that would witness Al-Mahdi's bay'ah alone. It was drawn for every generation between then and now — for the generation of the companions who first heard it, for the generation of the early scholars who systematized it, for the generation of Ibn Kathir who wrote Al-Nihayah in the midst of the Mongol devastation, for the generation of al-Albani who authenticated its narrations in the midst of 20th-century ideological chaos, and for the generation reading this book in the midst of the 21st century's particular combination of technological power and moral disorientation.

> *How blessed are the strangers — those righteous people who are few among many corrupt ones, and those who disobey them are more numerous than those who obey them.*
>
> **— Musnad Ahmad, Hadith 6650 — Sahih according to al-Albani**

The Prophet's description of the blessed strangers — al-ghuraba, the forerunners who live according to the truth in a world that has drifted from it — is the tradition's final word to the person living in the period of sign accumulation. You are not wrong. Your moral seriousness is not excessive. Your investment in depth when the environment rewards surface is not naivety. Your maintenance of genuine covenant when the world has institutionalized its violation is not idealism. It is precisely what the tradition identifies as the quality that the era of the accumulation demands — and the quality that makes you, in the prophetic vocabulary, blessed.

> إِنَّ الَّذِينَ آمَنُوا وَعَمِلُوا الصَّالِحَاتِ سَيَجْعَلُ لَهُمُ الرَّحْمَٰنُ وُدًّا
>
> *Inna alladhina amanu wa 'amilu al-salihati sayaj'alu lahumu al-Rahmanu wudda*
>
> *"Indeed, those who have believed and done righteous deeds — the Most Merciful will appoint for them affection."*
>
> **Surah Maryam, 19:96**

The final Quranic verse of this book is from Surah Maryam — the surah named for the mother of Isa ibn Maryam, the figure whose return is the End Times sequence's penultimate correction. Its promise is both intimate and comprehensive: for those who believe and do righteous deeds, the Most Merciful — al-Rahman, the attribute of divine mercy that encompasses all of creation — will appoint wudd: deep, settled, abiding affection. Not merely reward in the accounting. Affection in the divine relationship. The merciful God of the End Times sequence — who sends the gentle wind to collect the mustard seed, who preserves Isa alive for the world's final need, who destroys Gog and Magog with a worm so that no human is required to risk their life against the unresistable — is the same Merciful God who appoints deep affection for those who choose truth and righteousness in the measures before the coda.

> *For every reader who closes this book carrying something they did not carry when they opened it — a clearer picture, a more honest relationship with the tradition, a renewed sense that the framework of their faith has the analytical depth to meet the actual complexity of the world they inhabit — the journey has been worth the ten chapters. The roadmap is complete. The traveling continues.*

The Road Behind, the Road Ahead

The roadmap of Al-Mahdi in the End Times is complete. Al-Mahdi will emerge. The Dajjal will appear and be defeated. Isa ibn Maryam will descend and govern. Gog and Magog will be released and destroyed. The remaining signs will close the testing environment. The trumpet will sound. The accounting will begin. Every soul will find, in that accounting, the precise and complete record of what it chose in the time it was given.

None of that is contingent on whether you read this book, or believed its arguments, or changed your life because of it. The sequence will complete regardless. What is contingent — what has always been contingent, since the first human being was placed on the earth with the capacity for moral choice — is the quality of what you bring to the accounting. The tradition does not promise that quality will be comfortable to develop. The burning coal is real. The social cost of integrity in an era of moral inversion is real. The exhaustion of maintaining depth in a one-eyed world is real.

But the roadmap also tells you — and this is its final and most important word — that you are not navigating this alone, or in the dark, or without a framework that makes sense of the terrain. The Prophet Muhammad (peace be upon him) walked this road ahead of you, far enough ahead to see the whole of it, and he turned and described what he saw with a precision that fourteen centuries of scholarly transmission have preserved intact for this exact moment. The map is in your hands. The journey continues. The destination is certain.

Plant the tree. Recite Al-Kahf. Build the community. Maintain the amanah. Teach what you genuinely know. Love what is real. And when the weight of the signs feels heaviest — when the accumulation seems most irreversible and the correction most distant — remember that the most powerful force in the history of civilizational correction was a man who did not seek the role, standing between the Rukn and the Maqam, accepting what he could not refuse, with the hand of Allah over his hands and the trajectory of history bending toward the justice that was always its destination.

> *The road ahead is not longer than what has already been traveled. The correction is closer than it appears. And the*

> *preparation required — a mustard seed of genuine faith, a genuine orientation toward justice, a genuine love of truth — is precisely what you have been building in every honest moment of your life. Do not stop building it.*

The roadmap is complete.
The journey is not.
The destination is certain.
What remains is the quality of the traveling.

✦ ✦ ✦

سُبْحَانَكَ اللَّهُمَّ وَبِحَمْدِكَ أَشْهَدُ أَنْ لَا إِلَٰهَ إِلَّا أَنْتَ
أَسْتَغْفِرُكَ وَأَتُوبُ إِلَيْكَ

Glory be to You, O Allah, and praise. I bear witness that there is no god but You. I seek Your forgiveness and turn to You in repentance.

وَصَلَّى اللَّهُ عَلَى سَيِّدِنَا مُحَمَّدٍ وَعَلَى آلِهِ وَصَحْبِهِ وَسَلَّمَ

May Allah's blessings and peace be upon our Prophet Muhammad, his family, and his companions.

— END —

www.ingramcontent.com/pod-product-compliance
Lightning Source LLC
Chambersburg PA
CBHW050017170726
48282CB00025B/435
* 9 7 8 9 3 5 8 9 0 5 1 8 2 *